D0849223

The Ups and Downs of Radio-TV Regulation

FCC

The Ups and Downs of Radio-TV Regulation

WILLIAM B. RAY

Iowa State University Press / Ames

William B. Ray joined the Federal Communications Commission in 1961 as chief of the Complaints and Compliance Division of the Broadcast Bureau where he became a recognized authority on many aspects of broadcast law. In 1973 the commission presented him with one of the only two Special Achievement awards ever awarded by the commissioners. Retired from the commission in 1980, Mr. Ray has been a consultant on political broadcasting law.

© 1990 Iowa State University Press
All rights reserved

Manufactured in the United States of America

No part of this book may be reproduced in any form or by any electronic or mechanical means, including information storage and retrieval systems, without written permission from the publisher, except for brief passages quoted in a review.

OLD WESTBURY LIBRARY
KF 2765.1
.R 39
Copy 1

First edition 1990

Library of Congress Cataloging-in-Publication Data

Ray, William, 1908–
    FCC : the ups and downs of radio-TV regulation / William Ray.—1st ed.
        p. cm.
        Bibliography: p.
        Includes index.
        ISBN 0-8138-0227-X
        1. United States. Federal Communications Commission. 2. Radio—Law and legislation—United States. 3. Television—Law and legislation—United States.   I. Title.
    KF2765.1.R39   1990
    343.73099'45—dc20   89–15330
    [347.3039945]   CIP

TO ETOILE, BILL, AND BOB

Contents

Foreword

From a background of nearly two decades as an insider at the Federal Communications Commission (FCC), William Ray has written a most definitive exposé of political tampering and corruption at an important regulatory agency. From the standpoint of the functioning of the American democracy, the FCC is probably the most important regulatory body in our government because of its impact on communications—the lifeline of democracy.

The title of the book is accurate but deceiving in that it gives the impression this might be just another heavy technical study of the workings of the FCC. In fact, Ray has done a carefully documented and low-key exposé of the incestuous relationship that has existed between the broadcasting industry and government.

His book is explosive and clear in relating the details of this relationship from the days of the Hoover administration's fuss with flamboyant female evangelist Aimee Semple McPherson, through the raw politicism of the Franklin D. Roosevelt era and the subtle and crude scandals of the Eisenhower administration, through the deregulation of the Reagan administration, which Ray characterizes as "a national disgrace."

While Ray is clear and specific with his criticism of presidents and FCC members, he is also just as clear and specific in naming networks and network officials who willingly took part in the political deals with senators and congressmen (Republicans and Democrats) and the White House. He reviews in detail the manner in which Lyndon B. Johnson parlayed his political and network connections into a broadcasting empire valued at more than $50 million. He is equally detailed on the questionable conduct of former Representative Oren Harris, the Arkansas Democrat who was chairman of the House Commerce Oversight Subcommittee and who acquired an interest in a broadcasting company during the same time he was responsible for policing the FCC and the networks.

The major thrust of Ray's book is to expose the scandalous political tampering that has accompanied the federal government's regulation of broadcasting—even before the creation of the Federal Radio Commission, predecessor to the FCC.

However, there are highly amusing sections of the book that involve the problem of trying to draw rules and make decisions that protect the freedoms of speech and religion and also provide some protection for the public from the financial frauds that are consistently perpetrated by a few radio and television evangelists. Equally amusing are the sections of the book dealing with medical quackery and the constantly perplexing problem of trying to keep obscene material off the air while giving a free rein to expression in art and literature.

It is doubtful there is anyone with a better-prepared background who could write an in-depth examination of the work of the FCC and the whole history of the government's efforts to regulate broadcasting than William Ray. Ray was born on March 24, 1908, in the little county-seat town of Harrison, Arkansas. He grew up with the broadcasting industry. He worked for three years as a reporter for the *Louisville Courier-Journal* in Kentucky while attending college at the University of Louisville before moving to newspaper work in Chicago, where he attended the University of Chicago Law School for two years. Although he did not complete his law degree studies, he qualified and received a B.A. degree from the University of Chicago.

Ray joined the National Broadcasting Company in Chicago in 1933 in a public relations post but shortly moved into the news division and eventually became news director for NBC's midwestern division as well as participated in news division broadcasts. He left NBC for a brief period to own and operate a small radio station in Ames, Iowa, before accepting the invitation of FCC Chairman Newton N. Minow to become chief of the newly created Complaints and Compliance Division of the Broadcast Bureau. In that post he was presented with one of the only two Special Achievement awards given by the FCC. The award was given to Ray despite his frustration in trying to get evenhanded decisions from the theoretically independent, but highly politicized, regulatory commission.

Chief of the Complaints and Compliance Division was the ideal place for observing the internal decision-making process and studiously analyzing the results. Ray's office had responsibility for receiving and reviewing all complaints, for investigating those complaints and precedents, and for presenting the results to the FCC.

During his seventeen years as chief of the Complaints and Compliance Division, Ray had a professional reason to carefully review the history of the FCC to try to find a pattern in the precedents of licensing and disciplinary decisions. What he found was a pattern of decisions whipped by political winds in Republican and Democratic administrations.

In the two years he remained with the FCC after leaving the post as head of the Complaints and Compliance Division, Ray directed special studies on political broadcasting and on the fairness doctrine. This work added to his wealth of knowledge and balance with regard to the admittedly difficult task that any government agency faces in getting the radio and television industry to engage in self-regulation while facing competitive pressure to engage in frauds and distortions and to push the frontiers on obscenity.

Ray's more than thirty years in the news business gives him a sensitivity to the importance of the First Amendment rights to the media and the importance of keeping the government out of news judgments. However, his experience in investigating complaints against the broadcast industry has given him the greatest insight into how "the public interest, convenience and necessity" are often forgotten in the competitive striving for ratings and the financial greed that stimulated news distortions, frauds, and political chicanery.

Any citizen who is concerned about the power of television and what it has done, and is doing, to the society and particularly to the democratic processes of our nation should read Ray's book. The deregulation during the administration of Ronald Reagan is not the answer. Nor will the answer be found in the weak and politically warped regulation that permeated the preceding fifty years.

Other books have dealt with various aspects of the problem of regulating the industry. Some have been highly technical and aimed at those with special interests. Others have been sensational or have narrowly focused on the scandals of one specific era.

Having been personally involved in the investigation and reporting on the FCC scandals in the 1950s, 1960s, and 1970s, I have personal knowledge of many of the specific details of the congressional inquiries, what they documented, how they were aborted, and the general climate in which those inquiries were initiated. William Ray has dealt with those hearings in a low-key and objective manner and has included new insight based upon his personal observation as an insider with access to facts that were not available to journalists at the time.

—CLARK R. MOLLENHOFF

Acknowledgments

I wish to express appreciation, first of all, to Harry Heath, an old friend who now is Professor Emeritus at Oklahoma State University School of Journalism and Broadcasting. Without his counsel and assistance, this book probably never would have seen the light of day.

Thanks also are due to many others including Richard R. Kinney, Director of Iowa State University Press, and Bill Silag, Managing Editor; Sterling C. Quinlan, former Vice-President of the American Broadcasting Company; Henry Geller, Director, Washington Center for Public Policy Research; Andrew Schwartzmann, Executive Director, Media Access Project; Lawrence Bernstein, former FCC attorney; Harry A. Becker, veteran communications attorney; and Ray V. Hamilton, former network executive and station broker.

I am likewise indebted to Susan Hill, Librarian of the National Association of Broadcasters; Catherine Heinz, Director of the Broadcast Pioneers Library; J. Lamar Woodard, law librarian and professor of law, Stetson University College of Law; and the staff of the Federal Communications Commission library, for their cooperation.

Thanks also go to Sandra S. Wood of Fairfax, Virginia, for her expert typing of the manuscript.

Introduction

A member of the staff of the Federal Communications Commission (FCC) once said that the door to the commission's meeting room should consist of a large mirror. When he entered that room, he explained, he felt as if he were entering *Through the Looking Glass* because what took place inside reminded him of something that Lewis Carroll might have written.

There was some truth to this comment. The conduct of the FCC and its predecessor, the Federal Radio Commission, often has defied logic and sometimes has been scandalous, but in light of the agency's inherent deficiencies and the magnitude of its task, its record is perhaps as good as a realist might expect. Its members are appointed primarily for political reasons, and almost none has had any prior knowledge of the field of communications, yet they are charged with responsibility for regulating the most powerful medium of communications in all history in an era when "the medium is the message." The FCC is supposed to make sure that broadcasting stations serve the "public interest, convenience and necessity," but it is forbidden by law to exercise any form of censorship over the very programs through which these ends might be achieved. Newton N. Minow, a former FCC chairman, once wrote:

About the only guarantee given to an appointee to the FCC is that he will work in a jungle of procedural red tape that flowers wildly out of the quicksands of constantly changing public policy. This is a quixotic world of undefined terms, private pressures and tools unsuited to the work. The basic tool is the Communications Act itself. Its language is purposely vague and open to all kinds of interpretation. The FCC is supposed to look after the "public interest, convenience and necessity" but this term has never been satisfactorily defined.[1]

Although burdened with many handicaps, the commission is confronted with an almost insurmountable volume of work. It issues millions of licenses that it must periodically renew after determining, in theory, that each renewal will serve the public interest. It is responsible for regulating not only the broadcasting stations but all others as well, including citizens band, amateur, police and fire department, and cellular auto radios plus many other forms of electronic communication such as satellites, cable TV systems, and even the garage door opener down the street. Despite the enormousness of this task, Congress and the president reduced the number of commissioners from seven to five in 1983.

Small wonder, then, that the commission's actions sometimes have been bizarre. Some of them, bizarre and otherwise, are of particular interest and significance. The book does not purport to cover all aspects of broadcast regulation, nor is it intended as either an attack on or a defense of the commission. Some of the agency's actions are praised, others criticized, and an effort is made to set forth the reasoning underlying those that are criticized.

Cases are grouped by subject matter, beginning with those involving news twisting. Next come instances in which the commission fell victim to political pressure or manipulation including the first public revelation of the story behind the Don Burden case.

The chapter on obscene/indecent language reveals how the commission struggled for years to obtain definitions of these terms from the courts and finally succeeded.

The chapter on the little-understood fairness doctrine examines the development of this regulation and recent action by the commission to nullify it, over the protests of Congress.

In "The Radio Medicine Men" we go back to the days when quacks like Doctor Brinkley were using the airwaves to sell goat-gland operations and cancer cures. Radio preachers, the subject of the next chapter, have posed difficult problems for the commission for constitutional reasons, but its record here was for many years commendable. Then it whitewashed the Jim Bakker "Pearlygate" case.

Examples of the influence of Congress on the commission are given in the following chapter, and, finally, a summary is presented of the Ronald Reagan commission's efforts to undermine much of the basic concept of broadcast regulation.

Many of the facts herein never have been published before. Others have appeared only in law reports, trade journals, or transcripts of congressional hearings, none of which was readily available to the public. Still others such as the Brinkley case were publicized so long ago that most present-day readers know nothing about them.

It may be appropriate at this point to explain briefly how the commission came into existence and how it goes about enforcing the Communications Act.[2]

When radio broadcasting began in this country in 1920 the only statute governing it was the Radio Law of 1912, which authorized the secretary of commerce to license and, to a limited extent, regulate the dot-and-dash wireless communications to which radio was then limited. This statute proved utterly inadequate to control radio broadcasting. It was succeeded by the Radio Act of 1927, which created the Federal Radio Commission (FRC). Regulation of telephone and telegraph communication remained the province of the Interstate Commerce Commission under the Interstate Commerce Act of 1888.

Following the election of President Franklin D. Roosevelt in 1933, the Communications Act of 1934 was enacted, creating a Federal Communications Commission composed of seven commissioners appointed by the president "by and with the advice and consent of the Senate." The new commission was given responsibility for regulation of interstate and foreign communication by wire as well as by radio and thus took over the regulation of telephone and telegraph communication from the Interstate Commerce Commission.

Everyone who transmits any sound or image by radio or television must first obtain a license from the FCC. Nominally, its jurisdiction is limited to radio waves that cross state or national boundaries. However, as interpreted by the courts, it also covers signals that may originate in the center of a state and travel only a few blocks, because such signals might cause local interference to others coming from beyond the state's borders. Even diathermy machines and electronic garage door openers are in some ways subject to FCC regulation.

A station is licensed for a definite period of time and then must apply for renewal. Broadcasting stations formerly were licensed for three-year terms. Later, radio station license terms were extended to seven years and TV stations to five.

If a broadcast station appears to have violated the law during its license term, the commission may decide to grant it only a short-term, "probationary" renewal. If the commission thinks the violations were more serious, it may conduct a hearing to determine whether to renew the license at all or revoke it.

A hearing also will be ordered when another applicant for a station's frequency files "on top" of the station's renewal application, claiming that if given the license it would serve the public interest better than the incumbent licensee. When this happens a comparative hearing is held to determine which applicant is the better qualified.

Hearings are held before the commission's administrative law judges (ALJ), formerly called hearing examiners. At the end of a hearing the ALJ issues an initial decision, which becomes final unless appealed by either party to the commission. In some cases the appeal goes first to an intermediate panel called the Review Board, which consists of three high-ranking FCC staff members.

Major hearings usually are long and expensive. Cases may drag on for years and then be appealed to the U.S. circuit courts of appeal and possibly to the Supreme Court. The cost to the contending parties may run to millions of dollars in legal fees and related expenses. Designating an application for hearing is a form of punishment in itself, regardless of the outcome of the hearing.

In most cases the commission has another sanction available: the forfeiture. It may fine a station up to two thousand dollars for each day of violation but no more than twenty thousand dollars in total for "willful or repeated violation" of the Communications Act or the FCC's rules.

Finally, there is what some cynics say is the commission's favorite way of reacting to illegal behavior on the part of its licensees: the letter of admonition. It scolds the licensee and says not to do it again.

I hope that the following pages will provide some insight into the endless problems that the FCC has faced in the constantly changing field of electronic communications and how it has fared in trying to deal with them. As my colleagues at the agency often said, its initials in reality should stand for "From Crisis to Crisis."

The Ups and Downs of Radio-TV Regulation

1

News Distortion

The Columbia Broadcasting System (CBS) received a Peabody Foundation Award in 1969 for a documentary program titled "Hunger in America." The program opened with a heartrending scene of a doctor trying to revive an emaciated black infant. Off-camera, a CBS narrator intoned: "Hunger is always easy to recognize when it looks like this. This baby is dying of starvation. He was an American. Now he is dead."[1]

There was one thing wrong about this statement. It was false.

The baby was not a victim of malnutrition. He was born prematurely because his mother suffered a fall. Both parents were well nourished and moderately well-to-do. Their son had been born weighing only two pounds and twelve ounces. At the time CBS filmed him in a San Antonio, Texas, hospital he had just suffered a cardiac and respiratory arrest and was being resuscitated by a hospital physician. He died three days later. His death certificate listed the cause of death as "Septicemia. Due to Meningitis and Peritonitis. Due to Prematurity."[2] Hospital doctors explained that the premature birth was the original cause, which led to meningitis, peritonitis, and eventually, septicemia.

But in its search for a sensational opening scene, CBS did not bother to check the birth certificate or to interview the doctor who treated the baby; nor, according to hospital officials, did it ask them to consult their records in order to establish the baby's identity, even after the *San Antonio Express-News* had identified the infant and quoted his parents as saying that he had been born prematurely because of his mother's fall, not because of malnutrition.

CBS won another Peabody Award for a documentary called "The Selling of the Pentagon."[3] The entire program was slanted against the Defense Department, but the only part in which deliberate distortion was provable was a filmed interview with Assistant Secretary of Defense Daniel Z. Henkin by Roger Mudd, the CBS news reporter. CBS used trick film editing to misrepresent the actual sequence of questions and answers in this interview. Most of what Henkin said in response to one question was transposed to become his answer to another. Part of his answer to a third question was presented as if it had been his answer to a fourth. The Defense Department was able to prove these machinations because it had made its own audio recording of the interview. As Martin Mayer writes in *About Television,* "This episode clearly reveals a desire by the producers of the program that [Henkin] shall look bad on the home screen."[4]

These are but two of many examples of distortion or fabrication of news that are described in this chapter.

The Communications Act states that the FCC may renew a station's license only if it finds that "the public interest, convenience and necessity" will be served thereby.[5] The FCC itself has said, "Rigging or slanting of the news is a most heinous act against the public interest—indeed there is no act more harmful to the public's ability to handle its affairs."[6] The commission also has stated that "we shall act to protect the public interest in this most important aspect."[7]

But not a single station license has been taken away for this reason. In two cases the FCC has granted license renewals for less than the usual license period, which amounts to little more than a slap on the wrist. In all others it has managed to find reasons for doing nothing at all except to issue an occasional admonition.

The commission recognizes that broadcasting news and

other information is the most important service that radio and television can perform; in fact, it has said this is the principal justification for having allocated so much of the radio spectrum to broadcasting.[8] Then why has it been so timid in dealing with news faking?

The major reason appears to be an effort to avoid charges of censorship. This can be linked to repeated claims by CBS and NBC that any government inquiry into news broadcasting amounts to censorship or, at the very least, has "a chilling effect" on journalism. Some commissioners, reacting in panic to any accusation of censorship, have fled like frightened rabbits.

During the 1967–1971 period when many of the major cases of this kind arose and the precedents were established, the commission's general counsel was Henry Geller, who is currently director of the Washington Center for Public Policy Research. Geller, a brilliant attorney, had a great deal of influence over the commission. Many of its major policies were products of his thinking, including those dealing with news twisting. He was a hard-line regulator regarding most violations, but he tended to shy away from strict enforcement of the very policies he had recommended on news broadcasting, apparently fearing that the commission would be accused of censorship.

As a former broadcast news executive who at this time was an FCC division chief, I also was opposed to any effort by the government to control news reporting, but I believed that a deliberate effort by a licensee to distort news for its own benefit raised an entirely different question. The issue no longer was one of free exercise of news judgment but whether a broadcaster should be permitted to use a government grant (the license) for deliberate deception of the public for personal benefit. A licensee's right to report what was believed to be the truth, no matter how distasteful to the government, churches, big business, or any other part of the establishment, is not challenged.

The FCC's stated policies on news twisting are:

1. It will not try to decide whether a news report or commentary is "true" or "false." To do so would be to set itself up as "the national arbiter of the truth" and would amount to censorship.

2. "Staging" (fabrication) or deliberate distortion of news is against the public interest, but before taking action, the commission must have "extrinsic evidence" that the violation took place and that the owner or the top management of the station or network was responsible for it.[9]

What the FCC means by extrinsic evidence is direct testimony from someone in a position to know the facts (such as a writer or reporter) that the owner, manager, or news director of a station directed him or her to invent or distort a news item. The commission will not enter a case merely because it appears on the basis of what was broadcast that a news item *must* have been faked or slanted.

On the surface these policies are highly commendable. In practice, the commission has avoided real enforcement of them. Time after time, after denouncing news rigging or slanting as the most "heinous" sin of all, the commission has found some reason for doing nothing. The reason usually advanced is lack of proof that the deed was ordered by the owner or top management.

Curiously enough, the FCC has applied a stricter standard of licensee responsibility to less important violations. When a station has bilked its advertisers by issuing fraudulent bills or broadcast rigged contests, it has not been excused on the basis of a plea that the station owner didn't order the violation or even knew about it. In such cases the commission has ruled that the owner must "exercise adequate supervision and control" over the station and that he or she will be punished even if not aware of the violations.

When it took away the license of Station KRLA, Pasadena, California, in 1962, for example, the commission rejected the licensee's claim that its ignorance of a fraudulent contest on the station should absolve it of responsibility. It said

Inherent in such a contention . . . is the view that a licensee who delegates to persons it deems responsible, authority to operate and manage a station cannot be held responsible for their activities if it is unaware of them. This is, of course, a completely untenable view. Retention of effective control by a licensee of a station's management and operations is a fundamental obligation of the licensee, and a licensee's lack of familiarity with station operation and management may reflect an indifference tantamount to lack of control.[10]

The commission has denied many other licenses on the basis of the same reasoning including those of KWK, St. Louis, in 1963[11] and WNJR, Newark, in 1969.[12] In the WNJR case it emphasized that "a multiple station owner, or an absentee owner, is subject to the same degree of responsibility for adequate supervision over operation as a local owner who is integrated in ownership and management. To hold otherwise would result in giving an added benefit to absentee ownership as compared to local ownership."[13]

But when it comes to violations involving news programs, the FCC's strictness dissolves. The licensee is sent a mild reprimand for inadequate supervision of employees, unless the licensee itself can be proved to have ordered the violation. Even when principals of a station or network have been proven to be responsible, the worst punishment imposed has been a rap on the knuckles.

The two cases cited at the beginning of this chapter are examples of how the commission has applied its policy. Let us examine them in further detail.

Hunger in America

The Columbia Broadcasting System gave FCC investigators the following account of the filming of the baby in the San Antonio hospital.

On the date in question the crew was filming scenes in the nursery for premature babies. Martin Carr, producer of the program, later stated that a hospital pediatrician, Dr. Elliott Weser, told him that most of the babies in the ward were suffering from malnutrition. Vera Burke, who was in charge of social services at the hospital and who acted as the hospital's liaison with CBS, told Carr there was a high incidence of premature babies in the ward because of malnutrition in the mothers.

While the crew was in the nursery, a cameraman noticed that one infant had stopped breathing. A doctor was called who resuscitated the baby. The cameraman filmed the entire episode.

Carr said he was told later by Burke that the baby they had filmed had died of malnutrition. He also said that after the San Antonio newspaper story appeared, he asked Burke and Dr. Weser whether the hospital records could settle the question as to whether the baby had died of malnutrition. Carr stated that Burke answered that the records no longer were available and that Dr. Weser said it would be difficult to prove anything by them.

When interviewed by FCC investigators, however, Burke denied she had told Carr or anyone else that the baby had died of malnutrition. She merely said the baby had died.

As for Carr's claims to have called Burke and Dr. Weser about checking the hospital records, both denied that he had asked them to do so.

In any event, it was hard for the FCC to understand why Burke or the doctor would have said the records were not available or that it would be difficult to prove anything by them. The FCC investigators were given ready access to the records. An examination of them and consultation with the record librarian established that none of the six babies who died in the nursery during the eleven-day period surrounding the filming of the infant and its death had suffered from malnutrition. Two of the infants who died were girls and thus could not have been the one filmed. Two others died before the day the film was shot. The fifth was of normal birth and weighed seven pounds. This left only Claude Wayne Wright, Jr., weighing two pounds and twelve ounces. Dr. Luis Montemayer, the physician who resuscitated the baby on camera, told FCC investigators that CBS was wrong in stating that the baby died of hunger. He also said there was no doubt that the baby shown on television was the Wright baby.

In its decision on this case, the FCC declared that "no further action is warranted here with respect to the issue of slanting the news." The question, it said, was whether CBS "engaged in 'sloppy' journalism or was recklessly indifferent to the truth in not ascertaining the cause of death of the Wright baby." Although the decision noted that there was a conflict between the statements of the CBS producer and members of the hospital staff, it stated that it would be "inappropriate" to hold an evidentiary hearing to learn who was lying and who was telling the truth (although that is why evidentiary hearings are held). In any event, said the commission, there was no extrinsic evidence of deliberate slanting of the news under orders from "the licensee or management."[14]

There was, of course, no evidence that William S. Paley, chairman of the CBS board, or Frank Stanton, network president, personally ordered the Wright baby to be falsely identified as a victim of malnutrition.

The Selling of the Pentagon

The basic facts of this case were related at the beginning of this chapter. The FCC's decision, however, may be of interest in illustrating the processes of reasoning by which it avoids enforcing its policies in this field.

Faced with documented evidence of deliberate distortion of Henkin's answers to Mudd's questions, the commission did not ask CBS who the culprit was or at whose orders he had acted. Had the news director or someone else at a similar level been responsible, the case would have confronted the commission with precisely the situation in which it had so often said it would take action. But rather than venture into an investigation that might force it to act, the FCC decided that it had no documentary evidence of deliberate distortion, although it had documents that established such distortion beyond doubt—the transcripts of the interview as edited and broadcast by CBS and as recorded on audiotape by the Defense Department. Specifically, the commission said, "Lacking extrinsic evidence or documents that in their face reflect deliberate distortion, we believe that this government licensing agency cannot properly intervene."[15]

The FCC seemed somewhat troubled by the case, however. Its decision went on as follows:

> We have allocated so much spectrum space to broadcasting precisely because of the contribution it can make to an informed public. Thus it follows inevitably that broadcasters must discharge that function responsibly, without deliberate distortion or slanting. The nation depends on broadcasting, and increasingly on television, *fairly* to illumine the news.
>
> We particularly urge the need for good-faith, earnest self-examination. In our view, broadcast journalists should demonstrate a positive inclination to respond to serious criticism. . . .
>
> It seems to us that CBS has failed to address the question raised as to splicing answers to a variety of questions as a way of creating a new "answer" to a single question. The very use of a "Question and Answer" format would seem to encourage the viewer to believe that a particular answer follows from the question preceding.[16]

Thus, the commission confined itself to a plea that the offender engage in "self-examination."

In the face of incontrovertible evidence of its distortion of the Henkin interview, CBS elected to stonewall and deny that anything wrong had been done. President Frank Stanton testified before a congressional committee that the interview had been "fairly edited." CBS News President Richard Salant claimed that the handling of the matter was "in accordance with customary journalistic practice."[17]

In an apparent effort to cool congressional anger and avert possible FCC censure, Stanton released a memorandum to staff on June 28, 1971, titled "CBS Operating Standards: News and Public Affairs."[18] The document obviously resulted from the Pentagon case but Stanton made no mention of it, and the memo did not even acknowledge that his memo represented any change in CBS news policies. Instead, it sought to create the impression that CBS *always* had applied strict standards "to assure that the programs produced by CBS News are actually what they purport to be." Stanton quoted approvingly a memo sent to the staff many years earlier by Salant.

There shall be *no* recreation, *no* staging, *no* production technique that would give the viewer an impression of any fact other than the actual fact, no matter how minor or seemingly inconsequential. . . . Anything which gives the viewer an impression of time, place, event or person other than the actual fact as it is being recorded and broadcast cannot be tolerated.

Stanton then laid down the current news standards. One dealt with filming a news event. He said, "It is essential that CBS personnel do not stage, or contribute to the staging — however slight — of any news event or story. Specifically, nothing shall be done that creates an erroneous impression of time, place, event, person or fact."

At another point, Stanton wrote, "If the answer to an interview question, as that answer appears in the broadcast, is derived, in part or in whole, from the answers to other questions, the broadcast will so indicate."

In fairness to CBS, it should be pointed out that its successful "60 Minutes," a program of investigative reporting, has, to the author's best knowledge, been free of the practices that characterized the "Hunger" and "Pentagon" programs.

The Richards Case

The first and most blatant case of news distortion to come before the commission took place more than twenty years earlier than the two just reviewed. It was the so-called Richards Case, which arose in 1948 and is cited in the law reports as *KMPC, Station of the Stars.*[19]

G. A. (Dick) Richards, a hard-shell conservative if there ever was one, owned three profitable radio stations: WJR, Detroit; WGAR, Cleveland; and KMPC, Los Angeles.

The commission received a complaint from the Radio News Club of Hollywood, of which the late Chet Huntley was president. The complaint alleged that Richards was forcing the news staff of KMPC to distort and suppress news; in fact, that he had fired several employees for refusing to obey such orders. The hearing on the case later revealed that Richards's directives to his staff had included the following:

1. Slant all news in favor of the Republican party and against the Democrats.
2. Present General Douglas MacArthur in the most favorable light and omit all references to his advanced age or deteriorating health. (MacArthur was Richards's choice for the 1948 GOP presidential nomination.)
3. Refer to President Truman as a "pipsqueak."
4. Always link the name of Henry A. Wallace, former vice-president and now the 1948 presidential candidate of the Progressive party, with communism. Refer to Wallace personally as a "screwball," "tumbleweed," "pinhead," or "pig-boy."
5. Use no favorable news about the family of the late Franklin Delano Roosevelt and "certain minority groups" (meaning Jews, who Richards believed were "susceptible to communism").
6. Make no unfavorable mention of the Ku Klux Klan.
7. Use, as unattributed "news," editorials chosen by Richards from current newspapers that reflected his views.
8. Use excerpts from Westbrook Pegler's syndicated column in the same way.[20]

The FCC ordered a hearing to determine whether the licenses of the Richards stations should be renewed. The hearing was long and bitter. Halfway through, the hearing examiner died. A new hearing began. Before the case could reach a final decision, Richards himself died. His widow petitioned the commission to drop the case on the grounds that she, the heir to the stations, had committed none of the actions charged against her late husband and that she would make sure they did not recur. The commission decided that with the death of Richards the issues had become moot and closed out the case.

Although this case never reached a final decision, it was of considerable significance since it indicated that the FCC would consider denying license renewal to a station if the owner suppressed or distorted news to serve private interests or prejudices.

The Richards case was not the first in which a radio licensee interfered with news content. It merely was the first major case to come to the FCC's attention.

Back in the 1930s WLW, Cincinnati, then the most powerful station in the United States because of a five hundred–kilowatt experimental power grant, hired Norman Corwin as a newswriter. Corwin later was to become well known as an author of radio dramas and documentaries. Soon after going to work at WLW for the then princely salary of fifty dollars a week, Corwin began receiving memos from management directing him not to mention labor disputes in the news. Corwin sent back a memo pointing out that omission of all news of an important local strike that was being featured on the front pages of the newspapers could cause listeners to lose confidence in WLW. The station's response was to fire him.[21]

It was not until almost two decades after the KMPC case that the commission again became involved in news distortion.

The WBBM Pot Party

WBBM-TV (Chicago) is owned and operated by the Columbia Broadcasting System. In 1967 it was running behind the local NBC and ABC stations in the audience ratings of local 10 P.M. news programs. Whether for this reason or others, WBBM-TV executives decided to broadcast reports on two successive news programs about marijuana smoking by Northwestern University students in suburban Evanston. John Missett, a young reporter recently graduated from the Northwestern University journalism school, persuaded the news editor to embark on this project. He said he believed he could get himself invited to a student marijuana party and obtain permission to film it for broadcasting. The pot party was duly held and filmed. Portions of it were telecast in November 1967.

Northwestern University complained to the FCC that the marijuana party had been "staged" by WBBM-TV in order to broadcast it and that the broadcast had been false in stating that the party took place on campus. CBS denied both allegations. (The party actually took place in a private home near the campus.)

In part because the Complaints and Compliance Division of the FCC then had only three field investigators, the field investigation of the case did not get under way until January. At that time investigators found enough evidence to cause the commission to authorize a formal inquiry, so that witnesses could be subpoenaed, questioned under oath, and, if it were deemed advisable, granted immunity from federal prosecution. (One student who had taken part in the party said he would give information only if granted immunity.)

The formal inquiry had to be postponed for several months because of the tactics of Congressman John Moss of California, acting chairman of the Subcommittee on Investigations of the House Commerce Committee. Moss became fearful that the FCC's inquiry would embarrass the subcommittee, which previously had made a cursory inquiry into the pot party case and then had dropped it. When he learned that the FCC was about to launch a formal inquiry, Moss hastily instituted one of his own. He placed all potential witnesses under congressional subpoena and ordered them not to talk to FCC investigators.

The commission eventually was able to conduct its inquiry. It found that Missett did indeed induce the holding of the pot party. The FCC report faulted CBS for not having supervised the young reporter closely to make sure that he was not staging the party for the purpose of filming it. The report also criticized the network for having no clear policies on investigative journalism.[22] Aside from these admonitions, the commission took no action. It had not yet formulated its policies on the need for extrinsic evidence of staging or deliberate distortion at the behest of top management.

The 1968 Democratic National Convention

The first national political convention to be broadcast in this country was the memorable 1924 Democratic National Convention in New York, which dragged on for weeks while early radio listeners heard the Alabama delegation time after time casting "twenty-four votes for Oscar W. Underwood," its favorite son.

The first convention to draw a large number of complaints against broadcast news coverage was the 1968 Democratic National Convention in Chicago. The principal charge was that the TV networks had slanted their coverage to favor the mobs of hippies that beset the city. It was alleged that the networks had not shown the mobs stoning the police but had made sure to broadcast every instance of the sometimes violent police reactions to these provocations. Complaints also were received that the news and commentary had been slanted against the administration's policies on the war in Vietnam. Finally, the FCC received information about four specific instances of alleged staging of news events.

The complaints against one-sided coverage fell under the fairness doctrine, which required that a broadcaster who presented one side of a controversial issue of public importance make an effort to present contrasting views on the issue. Each network responded to FCC inquiry with statistics on the amount of time devoted to each side of the hippy-police and Vietnam War issues, statistics that, on their face, indicated that the networks had given reasonable opportunity for presentation of both sides of the issues.

In view of the many hours each network had broadcast from the convention and the variety of scenes, personalities, and viewpoints presented, the FCC chose not to review the videotapes of the coverage itself, and thus it had to accept the claims of the networks that they were blameless. The task of reviewing a full week's tapes from each of the networks would have been endless and largely futile, since it would have called for a judgment of whether each portion of the massive news coverage tended to support one side of a controversial issue or another. More important, such an effort by a government agency would have come close to censorship, because it often would have amounted to an assessment of news judgment. If proponents of one side of a controversial issue are more active than the other in "making news," who is to blame television news editors if they give that side more exposure on the air? This is why the fairness doctrine rarely can be enforced in connection with news broadcasting, especially when broadcasts cover a considerable period of time.

In regard to staging charges, the commission asked the networks to make their own investigations of four reported incidents during the convention. They were:

1. A U.S. senator and his wife saw a newsreel crew in Grant Park arrange to have a young woman (wearing a bandage around her forehead as in "Spirit of '76") walk up to a line of National Guard troops and, when the newsreel crew gave her a cue, begin shouting, "Don't hit me! Don't hit me!"

2. Thomas A. Foran, U.S. attorney for the northern district of Illinois, witnessed the following incident near the Logan Statue in Grant Park: A man was sitting on the grass with his back against a tree, holding a large bandage in his hand and talking to a three-man camera crew, one of whom had a CBS trademark on his jacket. When the man held the bandage up to his head, the crew began filming. Foran approached and asked what they were doing. The camera team walked away and the man with the bandage cursed Foran and left. No injury was visible on his head.

3. An assistant U.S. attorney and an assistant corporation counsel of Chicago were in Lincoln Park on the evening of August 25 when they saw a man lying on the ground being filmed by a crew whose equipment bore CBS logos. Two young women dressed as nurses appeared to be giving first aid to the man. The film crew seemed to be giving verbal instructions to the two "nurses" during the filming. After several minutes the camera lights went off and the "injured" man jumped up and began talking to the crew. He showed no signs of injury.

4. Foran and one of his assistants witnessed the following

in Michigan Avenue in front of the Hilton Hotel on the night of August 28: After a confrontation between demonstrators and police, the demonstrators retreated slowly northward in the street, followed by a line of police. Behind the police line, a newsman was kicking pieces of burning trash into a pile in the street. Several cameramen were watching him. After he had a small fire burning, he was handed a sign that read, "Welcome to Chicago." He placed the sign on the fire and signaled to the cameramen, who began filming the burning sign.

In answer to the commission's inquiry, CBS replied that its investigation had revealed no evidence that its employees had been involved in any of the incidents. CBS said there had been rumors that a free-lance Hollywood film crew was in Chicago shooting a purported documentary about the convention and that it was possible that such a crew could have used fake CBS insignia in order to get through police lines.

NBC said it had found no evidence that any of its employees were involved in any of the incidents.

ABC reported that it had found that one of its employees was responsible for the bonfire incident and that it had suspended him for sixty days, since staging of news was contrary to its policies.

The FCC decided to do nothing more about the four incidents, since it lacked positive proof that any network had committed the first three and ABC had taken steps to discourage repetition of the fourth by suspending the responsible employee.[23]

ABC and CBS Become Sports Promoters

Entirely different kinds of questionable news practices came to the commission's attention in 1978 when ABC and CBS decided to stage their own sports events in addition to televising those produced by others. Neither the CBS tennis matches nor the boxing tournament staged by ABC was "fixed," but the FCC ultimately decided that both were misrepresented to the public.

CBS paid $500,000 per match for TV rights to its Heavyweight Championship of Tennis. This program series consisted of successive matches between Jimmy Connors and four other stars of the day: Rod Laver, John Newcombe, Manuel Orantes, and Ilie Nastase.

In addition to the half million dollars from CBS, the promoter of the Connors-Newcombe match, for example, received $300,000 from Caesar's Palace in Las Vegas, where the match was played, plus $200,000 in ancillary rights – a total of about a million dollars. Of this, Connors was paid $450,000 and Newcombe $280,000 – win or lose. But that wasn't the way CBS advertised the payoff on the air and in its newspaper ads.

Robert Wussler, then vice-president of CBS in charge of sports and soon to become president of CBS television, decided that it would be offensive to the public (in fact, "obscene") if it were told that a tennis player was getting that much for one match. So CBS announced that the matches would be "winner take all" for a prize of $250,000 per match.

In fact, the remainder of the prize was paid to the players secretly as "appearance money." In each of the last three matches (Connors vs. Newcombe, Orantes, and Nastase) there was no "prize" element at all, since compensation to the players did not depend on the outcome of the match (with the minor exception that Orantes would have received $300,000 instead of $250,000 if he had won). Win, lose, or draw, Connors was to get half a million dollars for each of the third and fourth matches.

CBS officials were well aware of all of this, the FCC found, but

despite such knowledge, the phrase "winner-take-all" or similar references to competition for a $250,000 winner's prize were used by CBS on numerous occasions in pre-match publicity, advertising, or over-the-air descriptions of three of the four matches without an accompanying disclosure that both players would receive substantial amounts of "appearance money." In our view, these references constituted false or misleading statements to the public.

The FCC was even more perturbed at learning that either Wussler or Barry Frank, who succeeded him as vice-president for sports, had lied to the commission's investigators. Here was a case of deliberate misrepresentation by a principal of the network, which could not be fobbed off on some underling. One of the FCC's concerns in this case was whether Section 317 of the Communications Act, requiring on-air disclosure of payments made for advertising, had been violated by CBS when it telecast plugs for Caesar's Palace without giving the required sponsorship identification. In its ruling on the case the commission stated, "We are very concerned over the new evidence contained in CBS' May 3 response, which disclosed for the first time that either Mr. Wussler, then President of the CBS network, or Mr. Frank, then Vice-President/Sports, had lied to the Commission investigators."[24]

The FCC became very irate about this (it has taken licenses away in times past for misrepresentations to the commission), but it did not become angry enough to take away any CBS station licenses. Instead it imposed only a token penalty on the network by granting a short-term license to the next one of its stations to come up for renewal. The reason given was that the case involved lies to the commission by *network management*. One would think that falsehoods by the management of a network were the worst kind, but the FCC suddenly found a soft spot in its heart for top network executives. It said their function "ordinarily requires little or no awareness of Commission policy concerning licensee responsibility in such nonprogramming-related areas as misrepresentations to the Commission"!

Also, said the FCC, it "rarely conducts field investigations of networks to obtain first person statements from management personnel [and] such persons are usually insulated by their law departments from direct contact with Commission staff."[25]

In other words, we at the FCC can't expect the managers of networks to realize it's wrong to lie to the commission, and although we may take away the licenses of small stations if their managers lie to us, we'll go easy on a CBS president and vice-president because our investigators talked directly to them and they were not "insulated by their law departments," as they usually are!

The commission sternly added, however, that "henceforth [but not *now*] misrepresentations by network personnel will be attributed to the licensee corporation operating the network and could result in designation of one or more of its licenses for renewal or revocation hearing."[26]

ABC's fling at sports promotion was titled the United States Boxing Championship Tournament, which was supposed to produce professional fight champions in eight weight categories. The network agreed to pay Don King Productions, as promoter, two million dollars for exclusive coverage rights to the tournament and first refusal on the later fights of the winners. *Ring* magazine, the so-called Bible of Boxing, was to designate the top twelve fighters in each weight class, and Don King Productions would invite them to take part.

The first bouts were telecast on January 16, 1977. Three months later, ABC stopped carrying the tournament and announced it was hiring a special investigator to inquire into "irregularities" including allegations that *Ring* magazine had compiled "inaccurate" records of many of the fighters in the tournament.

This investigation and a later one also ordered by ABC revealed that *Ring* had been listing fictitious bouts in the magazine in order to justify ranking some boxers as eligible to take part in the tournament. The ABC inquiry also revealed that many of the best American boxers had refused to take part, either because members of the Don King organization demanded kickbacks or because King Productions demanded a right of first refusal of their services for future bouts in case they won. Actually, ABC had required a "first negotiation/first refusal" right in its contract with King Productions, so King could hardly be blamed for protecting himself with a similar demand on entrants. At any rate, the result was that some of the best fighters in the country refused to take part in the tournament, and it came to a sudden end.

The FCC faulted ABC for not having acted earlier to find out what was going on in its tournament but imposed no other penalty in view of the fact that the network had launched its own investigation before any government agency could do so and had scrapped the promotion upon learning of the abuses that were a part of it.[27]

The Shooting of the Polar Bear

ABC and NBC reporting has been relatively free of staged incidents, but early in 1971, NBC unwittingly broadcast a faked film sequence purporting to show the death of a polar bear.

The program was titled "Say Goodbye." Its message was that many forms of wildlife are in danger of extinction. One sequence showed two arctic hunters firing rifles from a helicopter at an unseen target. The film then cut to the scene of a mother polar bear apparently in the throes of death while her panic-stricken cubs ran around her in confusion.

In fact, the bear had not been killed. She had been tranquilized by a dart fired by an Alaskan game warden in the course of his duty of keeping tabs on the movements of polar bears. After he attached a coded tag to the bear's ear, she recovered consciousness and went on her way with the cubs.

The producer of the program, Wolper Productions, Inc., had excerpted the scene of the bear and her cubs from an official Alaskan wildlife film and at some other time and place had shot a scene of the two hunters firing rifles. By splicing the scenes together in what Wolper chose to call a montage, the film was made to create an entirely false impression.

NBC explained that it had no prior knowledge of the staging of the scene but that, as a result of it, the network was developing guidelines for future nature programs that were intended to prevent any more broadcasts of fake scenes.

On the basis of this response, the FCC dropped the case.[28]

KRON, WPIX, and WJIM

The commission received many complaints over the years alleging news distortion by individual stations. Most were not backed by extrinsic evidence and were dropped. Three did meet this test and hearings were held.

KRON-TV, San Francisco, is owned by the *San Francisco Chronicle*. Former newsroom employees complained that the manager of the station had ordered them to slant or suppress news about several suburban cities in order to curry favor with their officials and enhance the *Chronicle*'s chances of obtaining cable TV franchises.

At the hearing a reporter testified that he had been assigned to cover the Vallejo, California, area for KRON-TV and that he wanted to do an expose of the situation he found there, but that Harold See, manager of the station, told him this would be "unsuitable" because it might jeopardize the *Chronicle*'s cable TV interests in that area. It also was alleged that See ordered the news department to cover the "Chicken's Ball" at San Carlos to curry favor with local politicians because of the *Chronicle*'s application for a cable franchise, and that the KRON news director sent a memo to the assignment editor stating that a library dedication should be covered in South San Francisco because of cable interests.

See denied these charges, and the hearing examiner found that there was no "strong evidence" of some of the alleged practices and that the evidence, "though inconclusive," supported the manager's denial of others. The commission renewed the license.[29]

WPIX-TV is licensed to the *New York Daily News*. In 1969 the trade publication *Variety* published charges of former WPIX newsroom employees that there had been deliberate distortion of news on the station.

During the subsequent FCC hearing, former employees of the news department testified to many examples of news fakery and misrepresentation including the following:

1. A Defense Department film showing a new army tank

23

being tested at Fort Belvoir, Virginia, was described as a battle scene in Vietnam.

2. During the Russian invasion of Czechoslovakia in 1968, old library film of crowd scenes in Bucharest, Rumania, was presented as that day's film of current happenings in Prague, transmitted "via satellite." The voice of a reporter who spoke from Vienna was presented as originating in Prague. Other reports from Vienna also were described as coming from Prague or "the Czech border."

3. A University of Indiana professor named Max Putzel was described as "a Russian scholar" and his voice on a news program was labeled by WPIX as an "eyewitness account from Moscow" of reaction of Russian citizens to the Czech invasion. In reality Putzel was not a "Russian scholar" but a teacher of German literature; he was not speaking from Moscow but from Gary, Indiana, to which he had just returned after a tour of Russia with other American scholars. His cousin, the producer of the WPIX evening news program, had reached him in Gary by telephone and recorded his summary of what he had heard on the streets in Moscow about the invasion before he returned to this country.

4. There were scores of instances in which newsreels that had been filmed from one to six days earlier were described as covering events that had occurred "today." Film of Hubert Humphrey campaigning previously in one city was introduced as that day's film of his appearance in another. War scenes shot earlier in one part of Vietnam were identified as film of that day's action in another part.

Evidence at the hearing revealed the background of these practices. The WPIX-TV evening news program, which once had an acceptable audience rating and steady sponsorship, had declined in ratings after it lost its star anchorman. Its longtime sponsor abandoned it, and management decided something must be done to pep it up. Additional staff members were hired including a producer who, it seems, took to ordering writers to distort the news. Some of the writers protested. When rebuffed by the producer, they appealed to the manager of the news department and ultimately to the president of WPIX, Inc. The news director did nothing. The president of the station ordered an investigation, but only after word had leaked out that *Variety* was about to publish an article about the malefactions. The staff member who protested most vigorously about the news distortion, Nancy McCarthy, was fired. (Later her mother wrote a letter to the White House, which was forwarded to the FCC, stating that since her daughter had left WPIX, she could find no employment in New York. She apparently had been blacklisted.)

It should be noted that the complaining staff members had taken their objections to the manager of the news department. Under the commission's stated policy on this subject, the manager of a station's news department is a part of top management and the licensee itself will be held responsible for his or her actions if extrinsic evidence establishes deliberate distortion. Here there was an abundance of extrinsic evidence.

Nevertheless, the commission voted four to three to renew the license. The decision termed the examples of distortion "inaccurate embellishments concerning peripheral aspects of the news" or "presentational devices."[30]

Commissioners Joseph R. Fogarty, Charles Ferris, and Tyrone Brown dissented. "The majority's decision," they charged, "is insupportable in fact or law. . . . The majority's attempt to trivialize these incidents . . . ignores the fact that these abuses were so repeated over a period of many months as to constitute a regular station practice — a regular and repeated policy deliberately designed to deceive and mislead the public. . . . The majority's approach would sanction any number of licensee frauds upon the public."

The dissent asked whether the majority would dismiss as an unimportant "presentational device" a station's faking of helicopter traffic reports by having traffic information read from its studio over the recorded sound effect of a helicopter.[31]

WJIM-TV, Lansing, Michigan, was controlled by H. F. Gross and his family. In 1974 the FCC designated the renewal application for hearing on the basis of a complaint that Gross personally had ordered suppression of news in order to serve his private financial interests. He had written memoranda to two employees forbidding them to broadcast any news about an important tennis tournament being held at the Lansing Tennis Club because "those people owe us $1,500." Employees also complained that in newsreel coverage of city council meetings they had been ordered not to show pictures of some council members because they were opposing Gross's bid for a cable TV franchise.

The administrative law judge found that the evidence was "conflicting" about blacklisting council members, but that the existence of the two memos made undeniable the allegations about blacking out the tennis tournament.

The hearing revealed other damning evidence against the licensee. The FCC has a rule requiring disclosure that recorded material is being broadcast when "the element of time is of special significance." WJIM-TV had routinely used a videotape of its 6 P.M. weather report on its 11 P.M. news program without revealing that the second telecast was a taped rerun. The station claimed that it substituted a live weather report at 11 P.M. whenever the forecast significantly changed, but in one stretch of time the Weather Bureau had revised its forecast fifty-seven times between 6 and 11 P.M. whereas WJIM had changed the forecast only nine times.

The administrative law judge also found that WJIM-TV's sister AM station, WJIM, had issued maps to advertising prospects that misrepresented the area covered by its signal, a practice often denounced by the commission.

Finally, the hearing revealed that WJIM-TV repeatedly had deleted parts of CBS commercial television programs (including commercial messages) without notifying the network, thereby violating its network contract and obtaining reimbursement for material not carried. The FCC considers this a fraudulent billing practice. It has denied license renewals for fraudulent billing.

The judge's decision was to deny renewal of license." The appeal in this case went from the administrative law judge to the Review Board instead of going directly to the commissioners. The Review Board is composed of three upper-level staff members who rule on certain matters in order to relieve the commission of some of its adjudicatory duties.

In this case the Review Board evidently took its cue from the 1981 attitude of the commissioners toward law enforcement. It minimized the many WJIM violations and emphasized mitigating circumstances in order to justify a decision to grant a short-term license instead of denying renewal.[33] The commission affirmed this decision in October 1983 by a three-to-one vote.

Thus the FCC kept intact its do-nothing record in news cases. Some of the cases outlined in this chapter did not, of course, justify punitive action. For example, NBC did not know or have reason to suspect that the independent producer of the polar bear sequence had staged it. And when ABC belatedly discovered that an employee had contrived the sign-burning scene during the 1968 Democratic convention, it disciplined him. Moreover, ABC began its own investigation of the boxing tournament before the FCC entered the case.

However, the commission also chose to do nothing about "The Selling of the Pentagon" and "Hunger in America," and when confronted with the facts about the CBS tennis tournament, it imposed a minimal penalty.

Nor was the commission's tolerant attitude confined to the networks. In the KRON, WPIX, and WJIM cases it chose to minimize evidence harmful to the licensee and to emphasize that which cast doubt on the violations or mitigated their seriousness.

Any government regulation of news programming is likely to bring forth cries of censorship from some quarters. It might have been understandable if the FCC had chosen to wash its hands publicly of all complaints of news staging and distortion; at least its stated policy would have been consistent with its actions. Instead, it claimed to "protect the public interest in this most important aspect," but it has not done so.

News Twisting for Ideological Reasons

The preceding pages dealt with what might be termed corporate slanting or staging of news in pursuit of sensationalism, better audience ratings, or the private ends of station owners or advertisers. There is, however, a much more pervasive form of news twisting: that which is done by individual writers, editors, commentators, or producers to advance their personal ideologies. This form of distortion is much more common than the other and therefore considerably more harmful in its cumulative effect.

Most of those who slant the news on radio and television would deny they do so, and many would be sincere. There certainly is no communist conspiracy among American newspeople, as some believe. Those who slant the news act as individuals and usually are motivated by a desire to remake the world. A few lean to the political right, but the vast majority incline to the left. When once asked why so many television reporters were liberal in their outlook, David Brinkley offered this explanation: conservative-minded college students usually attend schools like the Harvard School of Business Administration or the Wharton School and then go into business; liberal-minded students are more likely to study journalism and enter the news field.

My own experience in hiring journalism school graduates tends to support this theory—most turned out to be politically liberal. In writing news of a presidential campaign, for example, they tended to believe that what the Democratic candidate said was newsworthy, but they found little worth reporting in the speeches of the Republican candidate. They were not consciously trying to slant the news. They were judging it according to their own political, economic, and social viewpoints.

Nor are journalistic neophytes the only ones who tailor the news to fit their purposes. Young journalists grow up to be old journalists. Many persons tend to become more conservative as they grow older, but some do not, especially those in the news business.

The methods used to color the news range from the obvious to the subtle. The very process of selecting which stories to include in a program is likely to be affected by the worldview of the editor or producer. The same influences affect his or her decision on how much time to allot to each item. And, of course, the way a story is written affords endless opportunity to favor one viewpoint and denigrate another. *Time* magazine used to describe persons its editors didn't like as "beady-eyed" or "ferret-faced." Few broadcasters are that blatant, but many are not without sin in choosing parts of speech. A person in disfavor is represented as "claiming" that a certain position is valid, whereas a favored spokesman "points out" the truth. There is an old illustration of such semantic manipulation: "I am firm. You are obstinate. He is a stubborn mule."

Network news reporters have gone far beyond such relatively innocuous verbal tricks as these. In her 1971 book *The News Twisters,* Edith Efron analyzed the evening newscasts of the three television networks for the last seven weeks of the 1968 presidential campaign. She found many varieties of verbal legerdemain, all aimed at promoting the ultraliberal viewpoint.

She wrote the following about one category she called "euphemisms":

This technique consists of using evasive terminology when discussing illegal, violent or criminal activities — always to the advantage of the practitioners of political violence. Violent mob outbreaks are called "demonstrations"; violent disruptions of people's right of free speech are called "protest"; violent assaults on persons are called "heckling"; violent provocations of police are called "confrontations" or "demonstrations"; violent assaults on property are called "liberating buildings"; thefts of property are called "commandeering"; acts of arson are described as "fire dances"; radicals shrieking abuse at candidates and threatening to destroy society are called "youth."

By omitting the correct legal and moral nomenclature the network reporter omits the critical opinion of organized society itself on such actions and tacitly communicates his sympathy for them.[34]

Among other types of news distortion cited by Efron was the use of "anonymous" sources of opinion. Instead of acknowledging that he is giving his own opinion, the news twister will say that "critics feel" or "observers point out" or "experts believe" or "it is widely thought" that something is true.

"These sources," Efron writes, "are totally uncheckable and must be taken on blind faith. . . . Not coincidentally, 'anonymous' sources *invariably* support liberal or Democratic or left causes; *never* the other side."[35]

As might have been expected, *The News Twisters* brought forth a chorus of denials from the TV networks. Richard Salant, then president of CBS News, led the attack on the book, perhaps because Efron's analysis indicated that CBS had been the worst sinner. Even before the book went on sale, Salant was issuing press releases attacking it and engaging research firms to prove that it was wrong. This activity led Efron to produce another volume in 1972 titled *How CBS Tried to Kill a Book.*

No matter how sincerely motivated or diligently pursued, however, her attempt to establish bias by analyzing transcripts of news programs could not prove conclusive because her results were based on subjective judgment of news. Some news items may clearly favor side A over side B and some may favor B over A, but inevitably many will be neutral in impact or subject to disputed interpretation. Efron tried to prove her point by statistics—and they overwhelmingly supported her thesis—but the statistics were based on her own evaluation of the news. The networks denied the accuracy of her statistics and managed to muddy the waters.

An even more important consideration is the need to recognize the relevance of news judgment. If in 1968 Candidate Hubert Humphrey made more speeches, cut more ribbons, and did more newsworthy things of other kinds than Candidate Richard Nixon, the TV news editors quite naturally would give more coverage to Humphrey than to Nixon. To criticize the ratio of Nixon items to Humphrey items was to quarrel with the editors' judgment of news values—always a slippery slope, at best. It was, of course, permissible for a critic to point out the disparity, but it was equally permissible for the networks to deny her conclusions.

News twisting sometimes takes the form of sly insertions of editorial comment in news stories. During the campus riots of the 1960s I once heard a network news report on a sheriff who reportedly had given orders to "shoot to kill" student rioters. The reporter concluded the item along these lines: "This is only one example, of course, but one cannot help wondering how many other sheriffs have issued similar orders."

Such a gratuitous comment could, of course, be appended to an item that reflected unfavorably on a member of any class of persons. If a black, a Jew, or a Hispanic were detected in a crime, the reporter could do his little bit toward smearing the entire group by adding that "one cannot help wondering how many other blacks [Jews, Hispanics] have been guilty of similar crimes." No network would permit the broadcast of such a smear of an ethnic group, but at that time law enforcement officials were considered to be fair game.

The news faking and distortion by broadcast licensees described in this chapter are violations of the public interest standard, which the Communications Act empowers the FCC to penalize, even though it has done little in that area. However, news twisting for ideological reasons by individuals poses a different problem, with which the commission cannot effectively deal. It has no licensing power over newswriters, commentators, or producers and it should not have such power. Moreover, the practices described herein often are too subtle to provide a basis for government regulation, even were such regulation legal or desirable. An effort of this kind would turn Uncle Sam into Big Brother, peering over the shoulders of members of the electronic news profession, perhaps objecting to the use of individual words or phrases or even voice inflections.

Material broadcast by individual commentators sometimes has caused the FCC to ask the licensees of their stations whether the licensees have afforded opportunity for contrasting views on the issues presented, in other parts of their program schedules. The author recalls a series of complaints the commission received years ago against WRAL-TV, Raleigh, North Carolina, alleging that the licensee was affording no opportunity for views in contrast to those consistently advocated by its daily commentator, Jesse Helms, but here the FCC was dealing with the licensee itself, in a situation quite different from that raised by sly news twisters. (There has never been anything sly about Jesse Helms, who later rode his TV reputation as an extreme conservative to election to the U.S. Senate.)

It must be concluded, therefore, that the only remedy for ideologically inspired news slanting by individuals lies within the power of their supervisors and that of the professional news organizations to which some of them belong. Individual protests by members of the public are notoriously ineffective.

The network presidents themselves are strong advocates of capitalism and have a great avidity for stock options. Yet so long as their programming yields hundreds of millions of dollars annually in profits they seem little concerned about the long-term effect on the public of the material they beam at it.

On the whole, the commission has done less to carry out its stated policies regarding news broadcasting than in any other field. It has recognized that this is the most important of all forms of programming because the public bases so many of its decisions at the polls and elsewhere on what it hears and sees on the air. However, after claiming repeatedly that it will "act to protect the public interest in this most important aspect," the FCC has done little or nothing.

NEW YORK INSTITUTE
OF TECHNOLOGY LIBRARY

2

Political Clout

Newton N. Minow, former FCC chairman, once wrote:

When I was Chairman, I heard from the Congress about as frequently as television commercials flash across the television screen.[1]

The role of political influence in broadcast regulation has long been recognized and is hardly surprising in view of the way in which federal communications commissioners are chosen and the fact that the agency is dependent on Congress for its continued existence. A considerable amount has been written on this subject but nothing about most of the examples that follow.

FDR Takes Care of His Friend Elzey

Although it is an independent agency, the FCC has been regarded by most presidents as simply another branch of the executive department and subject to their orders.

One of these presidents was Franklin Delano Roosevelt.

Although a majority of American voters supported him in four elections, most newspaper publishers did not. Roosevelt could see no reason why these unfriendly lords of the press should be allowed to own federally licensed radio stations. According to Eric Barnouw in his history of radio, *Tower of Babel*,[2] by 1940 more than one-third of all radio stations were owned or controlled by newspapers. In ninety-eight cities the only radio station was owned by the only newspaper giving the newspaper owner a virtual monopoly over dissemination of news.

When FDR appointed James Lawrence Fly chairman of the FCC in 1939, he directed Fly to break up the joint ownership of the two media. Fly never accomplished much in the area of dissolving newspaper-radio combinations. It was not until years later that the commission put any teeth into its intermittent efforts to diversify media control.

Roosevelt was more successful in another effort to influence the FCC. In 1935 the *St. Louis Star-Times* applied for a radio station that would be a competitor of KSD, owned by the *St. Louis Post-Dispatch*. KSD and WIL, another local station, filed objections to the *Star-Times'* application. The FCC designated the application for a hearing to determine whether the new station would cause interference to WIL and whether there was even any need for additional radio service in the area.

The FCC granted the *Star-Times* application in 1936 and the decision was affirmed by the U.S. Court of Appeals for the D.C. Circuit in 1937.[3] What never surfaced during the proceedings was the fact that when the application first was filed, Roosevelt made a telephone call to the chairman of the FCC, Anning S. Prall, that went something like this, according to Ray V. Hamilton who was present.[4]

FDR: Anning, my old friend Elzey Roberts is here in my office. Elzey is president of the *St. Louis Star-Times* and he wants a radio station for the newspaper.

Prall: Yes, Mr. President.

FDR: Anning, I want you to see to it that Elzey gets the station. Will you do that Anning?

Prall: I'll certainly do my best, Mr. President.

The *Star-Times* got the station.

"Hello World" Henderson and the Jesuits

One of the most colorful figures of early radio was W. K. "Hello World" Henderson, owner and general hell-raiser of station KWKH, Shreveport, Louisiana. In its heyday the station was so popular that readers of a national radio magazine voted it the most listened-to in the South.

"Hello World — don't go 'way-y-y" was Henderson's introduction to his own broadcasts, most of which were devoted to denunciation of his favorite devil, the chain stores. Chain store operators, he said, were "dirty, low-down daylight burglars" and "damnable, low-down thieves from Wall Street."[5]

Clarence Dill, an influential U.S. senator who was partially responsible for the enactment of the Radio Law of 1927, once happened to hear one of Henderson's harangues, typically peppered with expletives. Dill urged the Federal Radio Commission (FRC) to take action against him. It did, to the extent of giving him a probationary license renewal and extracting a promise of less cursing on the air in the future. But W. K. was not intimidated. He explained, "Hell, I have to cuss. My vocabulary is limited and I can't express myself unless I do."

He once concluded a particularly violent broadcast thus: "And if the Federal Radio Commission don't like that, it can kiss my ass (PAUSE), which is tied to the hitching-post outside the studio."

Like many stations in early broadcasting, KWKH shared time with another station on the same wavelength, in this case the desirable clear channel of 850 kilocycles. The other time-sharer was WWL, owned by Loyola University of New Orleans and operated by the Jesuits on its staff.

As usually occurred in such situations, each of the time-sharing stations eventually applied for full time on the frequency, precipitating a hearing before the Federal Radio Commission to determine whether either merited all or a greater share of the broadcast schedule.

Under ex parte rules that govern courts and other government bodies when holding formal hearings in adversary proceedings, a litigant is not allowed to communicate about a pending case with any of the decision-making officials unless the competing party also is present. If written material is submitted to the adjudicatory body, a copy must be served on the opposing party. Cases are supposed to be decided on the basis of the record of the trial or hearing.

If the old Federal Radio Commission ever heard of ex parte rules, it paid little heed to them. As soon as the WWL-KWKH hearing got under way in 1931, each of the competing stations set up a "hospitality suite" at a nearby hotel. One was at the Willard; the other at the Washington Hotel, a block away. According to one of the attorneys who represented WWL, members of the FRC and their aides partook freely of the food and drink offered at both suites, including bootleg liquor, since Prohibition still was in effect.

"The funniest part of it all to me," said George Smith, WWL counsel,[6] "was a little Jesuit priest who was a junior member of the WWL delegation and was sent to Baltimore every day to bring back a gunnysack of bootleg booze for the WWL suite. He was the angriest human being I ever knew, over being used in this way."

The hearing examiner gave the initial decision to WWL, awarding it sole possession of the 850-kilocycle channel.

Politics entered the case at this point in the persons of Franklin Delano Roosevelt and two Democratic senators. Roosevelt recently had been elected president, but the old Federal Radio Commission still was in existence pending establishment in 1934 of the Federal Communications Commission.

At that time, Senator Huey P. Long of Louisiana was broadcasting his homespun fireside chats over WWL. Senator Pat Harrison of Mississippi and Senate Majority Leader Joseph T. Robinson of Arkansas were outraged by Long's demagoguery, and since he was using WWL to spread his economic and social gospel, they went to the new president to see if something could be done to reverse the hearing examiner's pro-WWL decision. Roosevelt needed little urging. He, too, disliked Long and saw in him a potentially dangerous populist rival.

Roosevelt had influence over some members of the expiring radio commission because they hoped he would appoint them to the new FCC. Under pressure from FDR, the radio commission reversed the examiner's decision and voted in favor of KWKH.

But this was not to be the end of the case. The good Jesuits who operated WWL, hearing that Long's broadcasts were responsible for FDR's actions, told Huey to take his oratory elsewhere. Then they did some lobbying of their own. One powerful figure they approached was James Farley, manager of FDR's 1932 campaign, newly appointed postmaster general, influential adviser to the president, and a prominent Roman Catholic layman. The Jesuits convinced Farley that they had been done in. He took their case to the president and persuaded FDR to ask the commission to change the decision again. The commission did so. It assigned the 850-kilocycle channel to WWL full time and moved KWKH to the less desirable frequency of 1100 kilocycles.

"Hello World" Henderson probably never knew what hit him.

How Lyndon Johnson Got Rich

Many observers of the broadcasting scene have assumed that Lyndon B. Johnson's rise to wealth via ownership of radio and television stations beginning in 1943 was due solely to favoritism on the part of the Federal Communications Commission. Although the FCC did its part in helping the Johnson cause, the principal elements of his success were the willingness of the networks to do favors for him and his readiness to accept their favors while holding a public office that gave him power over them. The networks had a healthy respect for the political clout and personal ruthlessness of Johnson even while he still was in the House of Representatives, and his influence grew rapidly as he became senator, Senate minority leader, Senate majority leader, vice-president, and president.

The network executive who did most to aid the LBJ cause was Frank Stanton, a Ph.D. from Ohio State University who became president of CBS and one of broadcasting's most adroit operators. It was recognized in Washington broadcast circles that LBJ also got advice and assistance from NBC's Washington vice-president and chief lobbyist, Frank "Scoop" Russell.

Johnson also received helpful counsel from Sol Taishoff, publisher of *Broadcasting,* the largest and most influential trade publication in the field. When LBJ came to Washington in the 1930s — first as an aide to Texas congressman Richard Kleberg and then as a young representative — he was a neighbor of Taishoff and they became acquainted. In an interview years later, Taishoff said Johnson used to complain that he needed more income than the $10,000 he was paid as a representative. When Mrs. Johnson inherited some money, LBJ proposed buying a newspaper in Texas to augment his income, but Taishoff persuaded him that radio offered better opportunities for profitable investment.[7]

The Johnson rise to riches began with a small radio station in Austin, Texas, that had gone on the air in 1937 but hadn't done very well, in part because it could not persuade either CBS or NBC to make it an affiliate. In those pretelevision days network affiliation was as important to radio stations as it later became to television stations. Johnson learned that the station was about to change hands and persuaded the prospective purchasers to withdraw in his favor. As an inducement, he obtained an appointment to the U.S. Naval Academy for the son of one of them.[8] Thus, for the remarkably low price of $17,500 LBJ purchased the station in 1943 in the name of Mrs. Johnson. (He was to follow a pattern thereafter of putting his radio and TV stations in the names of his wife and daughters.)

Soon after Claudia T. Johnson became licensee of KTBC (later KLBJ) the Columbia Broadcasting System made it an affiliate and it began earning a profit. The FCC was happy to do its bit for the rising legislator, too. When Johnson bought the station it was authorized to operate only in daytime and it shared time on 1150 kilocycles with another station. Not long thereafter the FCC assigned it a much better frequency and authorized it to operate full time. Later the FCC also gave it more power.[9]

The profits from the Austin station were peanuts, however,

compared to the millions Johnson later made from television —
again with help from Stanton and Russell and a few assists from
the FCC.

The commission had frozen all further grants of TV licenses in 1948 after it became apparent that the original VHF
channels would not be sufficient to provide service for the entire
country. In 1952 the freeze ended with the release of a new table
of channel allocations that included UHF as well as VHF stations.[10] By this time it was pretty well recognized that a VHF
station in a populous area was going to become a gold mine.

The new allocation table assigned one commercial VHF
station to Austin, as well as one noncommercial UHF station.
Johnson quickly filed an application for the VHF channel. No
one submitted a competing application. As one observer later
remarked, this was not surprising in view of Johnson's political
clout. Filing a competing application would have been a waste
of money. At any rate, the FCC granted the Johnson application
as soon as possible, and the station went on the air on November 27, 1952. All four TV networks scrambled to grant it an
affiliation, so it could choose the most popular and profitable
programs from among them. The networks were ABC, CBS,
NBC, and DuMont. DuMont later went out of business.

The station enjoyed certain other advantages, too. A top
executive of *Broadcasting* magazine once told me that Stanton
had granted the station a higher rate of compensation for
broadcasting network commercial programs than CBS normally
paid affiliates in markets of similar size. He said he also had
heard that Stanton helped to persuade the American Telephone
and Telegraph Company (AT&T) to hasten the extension of its
coaxial cable circuit to Austin.

Whatever the case, while a number of other TV stations in
markets of similar or larger size were pining for direct cable
connections so they could carry network programs "live" rather
than by way of dim, delayed kinescopes, the LBJ station was
able to carry live telecasts of any network programs it might
choose. The 1952–53 *Broadcasting-Telecasting Yearbook* reveals
that the AT&T cable network to the Southwest ended at Dallas-
Fort Worth in July 1952, but shortly after the Austin station

went on the air, it was extended to Austin and on to San Antonio.

Two stations had been on the air in San Antonio since early 1950, but they were unable to get network connections until after the LBJ station began operating late in 1952.

At the time AT&T extended cable service to Austin, a number of other cities of the same or greater size were without network service, although each had one or more TV stations. They included Akron, Ohio; Spokane, Washington; Mobile, Alabama; El Paso, Texas; and Baton Rouge, Louisiana.[11]

Since UHF stations in those days were losing enterprises, Johnson had a TV monopoly in Austin for many years. Many other cities of that size had been allocated two VHF stations, but for reasons best known to itself, the FCC assigned only one to Austin. Moreover, the commission went out of its way to protect the Johnson monopoly in 1959. Although Corpus Christi, Texas, had two VHF stations at the time, the FCC decided to assign a third to it. The two existing stations protested that competition already was so keen that they were losing money and that the grant of a third license might bankrupt them. They suggested that the new station be assigned to Austin. Also, they pointed out, location of the new station in Corpus Christi would cause interference to a station that was about to be built across the border in Mexico. However, the FCC stubbornly adhered to its plan to give Corpus Christi a third station rather than to assign a second one to Austin.[12] It even went to the extent of persuading the Mexican government to relocate the newly planned station in that country so that there would be no interference problem.

After obtaining the Austin station, Johnson looked around for more TV worlds to conquer. The trouble was that others had gobbled up the more desirable VHF channels in Texas. But there is more than one way to skin a cat.

In Waco, M. N. "Buddy" Bostick had been granted a license for VHF Channel 10 and had launched KWTX-TV on April 3, 1955. Unfortunately for Bostick, CBS reneged on its promise to grant him a network affiliation for reasons that became apparent only later, and KWTX was left with no network. (ABC likewise refused him an affiliation, and NBC already had an affiliate in nearby Temple.)

Meanwhile, LBJ was busy contriving something. KANG-TV, a UHF station, had been established in Waco back in 1952 but had fared so badly (as did almost all UHF stations in those days) that it had been forced to go off the air in October 1953. Its network affiliations had been with ABC and DuMont. Nevertheless, in December 1954 Johnson bought the silent station for $115,000 and assumption of $19,000 in debts. CBS promptly decided that even though only a UHF station it would make an excellent Waco affiliate.[13]

This was a little too much for Bostick. He filed complaints with the antitrust division of the Department of Justice and with the Federal Communications Commission alleging monopolistic practices on the part of LBJ. Private negotiations began, in which Johnson personally took part. The result was a deal whereby Bostick agreed to give LBJ 29 percent of the KWTX-TV ownership in return for the worthless physical facilities of KANG-TV, and both CBS and ABC agreed to make KWTX-TV an affiliate. (Having served its role in the LBJ coup, KANG-TV then went off the air.)

Here is one more example of how the Johnson TV empire grew. In the 1952 allocation table, the city of Bryan, Texas, had been assigned a UHF channel. College Station, home of Texas A & M University, had been assigned VHF Channel 3 to be used by the university for a noncommercial educational station.

After Johnson acquired part ownership of KWTX Broadcasting Company, that corporation obtained a 50 percent interest in Brazos Broadcasting Company, which wanted to operate a VHF station in Bryan. The problem was that only a UHF channel was assigned to Bryan. It was decided to petition the FCC to switch its channel assignments so that the valuable VHF formerly assigned to Texas A & M would be reassigned to Bryan as a commercial channel, and Bryan's UHF channel would be given to the university as a sop. The FCC granted the petition and sought to justify its decision on the grounds that the university had not established a station in the four years that the VHF channel had been available to it.[14] (In some other localities the FCC held noncommercial channels open for longer periods so that a university or state legislature could raise or appropriate the money to build a station.) So with LBJ owning an interest in the new Bryan VHF station, it became affiliated with both CBS and ABC.

Johnson later acquired KRGV-TV in Weslaco, Texas, and several other stations. Even after selling off many of them in recent years, the LBJ Company, as it's now titled, still holds interests in three stations.

Two examples show the profits reaped by selling stations: the Austin TV station, for which Johnson paid nothing, was sold in 1973 for nine million dollars. The Weslaco station, which cost $175,000 in 1958, was sold three years later for $1,400,000. (Johnson's profits from TV and radio have been reported as totaling more than seventy million dollars.)

When Johnson succeeded John F. Kennedy as president, FCC staff members and commissioners expected him to sell his broadcast properties, since as president he would have authority to appoint members of the commission and would hold other powers over the agency that regulated the stations including veto power over its annual budget requests. Cohn & Marks, the LBJ law firm, told the FCC staff to get ready for an important announcement from the White House, but the announcement proved to be different from what had been expected. Instead of selling the stations, Johnson put them into a trusteeship. The trustees were old friends of the president.

Just how well he divorced himself from control and management of the broadcast properties is revealed in the following incidents, disclosed to me by editors of *Broadcasting* and *Television-Radio Age* magazines. Whenever there was a business matter to be discussed between CBS and the LBJ stations, Johnson would summon the appropriate CBS personnel to the White House to discuss it. Once he called Stanton in New York to complain that CBS was charging one of his TV stations too much for a syndicated program. Stanton told his staff to furnish the program to the station free.

When the president went to New York City to address the United Nations, he directed his national sales representative in New York to ride with him in his limousine from UN headquarters back to the airport. As soon as the sales rep got into the car, Johnson clapped him on the knee and asked, "Why haven't we sold those 10 P.M. station breaks [advertisements]?"

The Eisenhower Gang Hands Out the Plums

When the Federal Communications Commission ended its four-year freeze on grants of TV licenses in 1952, only 107 stations in sixty-four cities were on the air—all established before the freeze began.[15] Under the new table of allocations for the postfreeze period, more than 2,000 channels were made available in nearly 1,300 communities. Most of these were in the UHF range and some are vacant to this day because they were assigned to towns too small to support much more than a general store and a gasoline station. In fact, almost all of those who obtained UHF licenses in the 1950s went bankrupt because of the technical inferiority of UHF signals and, more importantly, because almost none of the sixteen million existing TV sets could receive UHF signals.

However, with hundreds of valuable VHF licenses to hand out and many more UHFs that the applicants *thought* would be valuable, the FCC was deluged with applications and was subjected to some of the most intense political pressure in its history.

The commission was so pressed to pass out TV licenses quickly that in uncontested cases, where there was as yet only one applicant for a license, it did not even give its staff time to put the facts and its recommendations in writing, as it always had in the past. Instead, the staff member who had examined the application was directed to stand up at a commission meeting and recite the facts as well as he or she could remember them, whereupon the commission would vote immediately on the grant of a license, which probably would be worth millions.[16] (One station has sold for more than five hundred million.)[17]

And did politics intrude in the selection of the grantees? As one FCC staff executive of that period said, "You bet your boots it did. With the Republicans out of power for twenty years and hundreds of multimillion dollar TV licenses to be handed out to deserving friends, what would you expect?"

The political clout that determined who would get the licenses was channeled through White House Chief of Staff Sherman Adams (of vicuna coat fame) and his White House aides. The FCC chairman and other amenable commissioners reportedly would get calls from Adams or a member of his staff that went something like this: "Mr. Chairman [or Commissioner] I hear that you're considering granting a license in Beaumont. I'd appreciate it if you would give consideration to the Perkins boys."

And the commissioner would make a note to vote for the Perkins' application, even though the case might be in comparative hearing between competing applicants and the commissioner was required by law to decide the case solely on the hearing record.

One staff member of the era recalls the time when the chairman forgot which applicant he was to vote for at a commission meeting and cast his ballot for the other. His legal assistant scurried up to the dais and whispered into his ear, and the chairman reversed his vote.

In his 1974 book *The Hundred-Million Dollar Lunch,* Sterling Quinlan quotes a former chairman of the FCC thus: "Let's face it. This was the Whorehouse Era of the Commission, when matters were *arranged,* not adjudicated."[18]

It should be explained at this point that in order to create standards by which competing applicants for licenses were to be judged, the FCC had established a number of criteria. They included:

1. *Local ownership.* Local ownership of stations was to be favored because it was believed that local owners would be more aware of and responsive to the needs of the community than would absentee owners.

2. *Integration of ownership and management.* The belief was that if the owner managed the station rather than delegating management to a staff that had no ownership interest, the station would be more likely to follow the licensee's stated policies and serve local interests.

3. *Diversification of media control.* Here the object was to avoid a monopoly over dissemination of news and opinion. If the same person or company owned the local newspaper, TV

station, and radio station, there would be less likelihood that a diversity of views on major public issues would be aired.

4. *Past performance.* If an applicant already had owned a station, his or her past performance might furnish clues as to how the new station would be operated.

5. *Proposed programming.* The commission examined the broad outline of an applicant's proposed programming to determine whether he or she could be expected to serve the community including minority groups, children, and such, as well as the bulk of the population.

6. *Broadcast experience.* In this category the commission considered the experience in broadcasting that an applicant might bring to the proposed station.[19]

Establishment of standards for comparing competing applicants obviously was necessary in order to bring some reason to the licensing process, but in practice it has enabled the commission to find justification for almost any decision it might arrive at. This is the way it goes:

If for some political reason the commission wishes to choose applicant A over applicant B even though A is an absentee owner with no integration of ownership and management, the commission will order its staff to write a decision justifying a grant to A. The staff will do so on the grounds that A has more broadcast experience, has an acceptable record of past performance, and proposes what the FCC chooses to think is better programming than B. B may be a local applicant with complete integration of ownership and management and may own no other station or newspaper in the city, but those who are hired to rationalize the commission's choices will play down these factors in writing the decision. In another case the staff may find it necessary to play up the same factors in order to justify a contrary decision.

The commission sometimes will tell its Office of Opinions and Review (OOR) which applicant is to be given a license without stating any reasons for its choice. The OOR then must use its ingenuity in trying to write an order that will justify the decision. I remember meeting Leonidas P. B. Emerson, then chief of the Office of Opinions and Review, in the FCC elevator one day after a closed commission meeting. He shook his head sadly and said, "They told us who is to get the license, but when I asked what their reasons were, Commissioner [Robert E.] Lee just said, 'Lonnie, you'll think of some.' "

Another example of how the FCC used its Office of Opinions and Review occurred in its award of a TV license in Jacksonville, Florida. In June 1956 it voted to give the license to Jacksonville Broadcasting Company. The Office of Opinions and Review dutifully wrote a hundred-page opinion supporting the decision. However, for undisclosed reasons the commission suddenly reversed itself and voted to award the license to a competing applicant, Florida-Georgia Television Company. The OOR staff then went back to work and came up with an equally long and elaborate decision that directly contradicted the previous one.[20]

In his book *The Professor and the Commissions,* Bernard Schwartz wrote that as of 1959

the FCC has decided some sixty television cases involving comparative hearings of mutually exclusive applicants. Analysis of these cases indicates a most disturbing inconsistency on the part of the Commission in applying its criteria. Whim and caprice seem to have been the guides rather than the application of settled law to the facts of the case. In effect the Commission juggles its criteria in particular cases so as to reach almost any decision it wishes and then orders its staff to draw up reasons to support the decision.[21]

Schwartz says that under the Eisenhower administration, eight outspokenly Republican newspapers had received TV licenses and ten Democratic newspapers had been denied them. He says no Republican papers lost comparative hearings except in cases where they were opposed by more powerful Republican interests. Conversely, no important paper that had supported Adlai Stevenson for president won a comparative TV case. This reminds me of a conversation I once had with the man who headed the Office of Opinions and Review in the early Eisenhower days. He said,

My God, they would grant a TV application to a newspaper in one city on the grounds that it was a local owner and therefore familiar with the needs of the area, and at the same time they would deny the application of a newspaper in another city on the grounds that the grant would bring about concentration of control of the media. Once they had two such contradictory decisions coming up for approval at the same meeting. I pleaded with them at least to take up the cases at different meetings so the Commission might not look so bad, but they wouldn't even do that. They acted on them both at the same meeting, giving entirely opposite reasons for the grants.

The Office of Opinions and Review must have been hard put at times to rationalize the awards, especially the grant of Channel 8, Petersburg, Virginia (WXEX-TV), to a staunch GOP supporter who really wanted to operate the station as if it were licensed to the larger city of Richmond and who practically told the commission so in his application.

The commission's *Sixth Report and Order,* which ended the freeze, assigned two VHF and two UHF channels to Richmond, Virginia, and allocated VHF Channel 8 to the smaller city of Petersburg, twenty-five miles south of Richmond. Originally the commission had been asked to assign this channel to Richmond rather than Petersburg, but in its *Sixth Report and Order* it declared that "no basis has been established on the record for the deletion of channel 8 assigned to Petersburg in order to assign that channel to Richmond. . . . Deletion of the sole VHF channel from Petersburg, a city of 35,000, in order to assign a third channel to Richmond . . . is in view of the circumstances unwarranted."[22]

But when politics entered the case, the commission gave Channel 8 to an applicant who eventually made it, to all intents and purposes, a Richmond station. In fact, it was allowed to identify itself as a "Richmond-Petersburg" station, and it is now listed under Richmond stations in the *Yearbook* of *Broadcasting* magazine.

How did this happen? There were two applicants for the Petersburg station. One was Southside Virginia Television Corporation, which promised to design programming primarily to serve Petersburg and the southern half of its coverage area, since two other VHFs and two UHFs had been assigned to serve the Richmond area to the north. The other applicant was Petersburg Television Corporation, which proposed to program for the more lucrative market of Richmond as well as the area around Petersburg. This must have sounded to the hearing examiner very much as if Petersburg Television Corporation was planning to operate the station for Richmond's benefit. So on this and other grounds—including the fact that Southside was owned by local Petersburg people, whereas the other applicant was absentee-owned—the examiner gave his decision to Southside. The examiner evidently didn't know or care about political realities at the FCC during the 1950s.

On the day before the commission was to vote to affirm or reverse the examiner's decision, Republican Commissioner Robert E. Lee, in company with Sol Taishoff (publisher of *Broadcasting* magazine) went on a little junket to Baltimore to inspect some stations there. To the best of my knowledge, inspections of stations by commissioners themselves, as contrasted to staff engineers, had ceased long before this time. Nevertheless, Lee later told two congressional committees that such was the sole purpose of his visit to Baltimore.

One of the stations he and Taishoff inspected that day happened to be owned by Thomas Tinsley, a leading supporter of President Eisenhower and a principal in Petersburg Television Corporation. Tinsley invited Lee and Taishoff to dinner that night. Lee's vote the next day was the deciding one in a three-to-two decision to overrule the hearing examiner and award the license to Tinsley's company.[23]

In order to justify the grant to an applicant that was absentee owned and obviously intended to serve the larger market of Richmond, the FCC's Office of Opinions and Review had to reach back to the Great Lakes Broadcasting Company[24] ruling of the old Federal Radio Commission. In the Great Lakes ruling each of three Chicago area stations was seeking a greater share of time on one frequency. Two were stations of general appeal. The third was operated by the head of a tiny religious sect who used his station's share of time to advance the strange tenets of that group. (See Chapter 6 for further discussion of Great Lakes.)

In turning down the application of this sect, the FRC said the station was being operated primarily for the purpose of propagating the creed of its owner and that the members of the faith and of the persons interested in it are extremely limited in number compared to those of other faiths, and it is not logical that such a sect should enjoy peculiar facilities for propagating its beliefs when there is not room in the ether for many other sects to have their separate stations.

It was in this sense that the radio commission said a station should serve its entire audience. However, the meaning of the decision was twisted by the Office of Opinions and Review in trying to justify an FCC decision to award a license reserved for Petersburg to an applicant whose purpose was to serve Richmond. The FCC sought to justify the grant by claiming that under the Great Lakes decision, "the entire listening public within the service area of a station . . . is entitled to service from a Petersburg station or stations." Thus, it distorted a precedent based on the *subject matter* of a station's programming to refer to the *geographical area* to be served.

Had the commission originally been concerned about giving Richmond additional TV service, its *Sixth Report and Order* would not have been so positive about assigning the channel to Petersburg and denying it to Richmond.

When word later leaked out about Lee's junket to Baltimore and dinner with Tinsley, the license renewal of Channel 8 was challenged and Lee was called before two congressional committees. He denied that he had discussed the Petersburg case over dinner that night and said he couldn't even remember how he voted on the case, a rather startling lapse of memory in view of the fact that his had been the deciding vote.

As for the FCC, after taking note of the congressional hearings, it decided not to reopen the Petersburg case.[25]

WXEX-TV was sold by Tinsley's company in 1967 for $7,150,000.

In his book Schwartz cites several other politically slanted license awards made by the FCC during the 1950s. In one, two applicants filed for a TV license in Madison, Wisconsin. One applicant was the *Capital Times,* published by William T. Evjue, a bitter opponent of the Eisenhower administration and of Senator Joseph McCarthy of Wisconsin. The *Capital Times* owned a radio station in Madison. The other applicant was Radio Wisconsin, which owned no newspaper in Madison but held a radio station there as well as five other AM, three FM, and three TV stations elsewhere in the region. Further, its largest stockholder controlled four major Wisconsin newspapers, three of which had strongly supported Senator McCarthy.

The FCC hearing examiner's initial decision awarded the Madison license to Evjue's newspaper, but the commission gave the license to Radio Wisconsin on the grounds that Evjue's ownership of both the Madison newspaper and radio station outweighed Radio Wisconsin's more extensive broadcast interest in the region.[26]

The FCC followed the same general line in denying a TV license in Sacramento, California, to the McClatchy newspapers because McClatchy owned two newspapers in Sacramento as well as newspapers and radio stations in other parts of central California.[27]

The Madison and Sacramento decisions were consistent with each other in relying on a policy against concentration of media control, but they were inconsistent with other decisions made during this period—the Channel 7 case and the Boston case.

Channel 7 was located in Miami, Florida. There were four applicants for Channel 7, three of which were owned by local citizens who had no other broadcast or newspaper interests. The fourth, Biscayne Television Corporation, had two principal owners, each of whom controlled one of Miami's two daily newspapers and each of whom also owned a Miami AM and FM station. Additionally, each had large radio and newspaper interests in other parts of the country. One of these men, John S. Knight, was publisher of the Republican *Miami Herald* and owner of a chain of Republican newspapers in Ohio.

The broadcast bureau recommended that the commission reject the Biscayne application because of concentration of control of the media, but in 1956 the commission awarded the license to Biscayne on the grounds that its principals had greater experience in the mass media![28] Of course, had the commission chosen to view common ownership of newspapers and radio and TV stations in this way, the Evjue and McClatchy cases would have been decided differently.

The commission's grant of a Boston TV license was even more startling. As in Miami, there were four principal applicants for the Boston channel.[29] Two consisted of local business and professional men with no other communications ties. A third was owned by nonresidents and held other TV interests. The fourth was the staunchly Republican *Boston Herald-Traveler*, which was the largest local morning and evening newspaper and owner of the principal AM and FM stations in Boston. The hearing examiner ruled out the *Herald* because of potential concentration of media control. He relied on the Madison, Wisconsin, decision for his precedent. He also noted that the *Herald* had used its ownership of the radio station in monopolistic ways such as selling combined advertising for the station and newspaper. (In other cases, the FCC had cited this as monopolistic and an unfair business practice.)

Further evidence against the *Herald* came in the form of an affidavit from its newspaper competitor, the *Boston Globe*. It alleged efforts had been made by the *Herald* to force the *Globe* to merge with it—efforts that allegedly included threats to use the prospective TV station to drive the *Globe* out of business if it rejected a merger.

In the face of all this, the commission reversed the hearing examiner and awarded the license to the *Herald-Traveler*. The decision was appealed as capricious and contrary to statute, commission policy, and commission precedent. The case dragged through the courts and the commission's processes for two decades. Then the commission reversed itself and awarded the license to another applicant.[30]

One fact that emerged during the proceedings was the existence of ex parte contacts with the chairman and other commissioners by the *Herald*'s publisher, Robert Choate, during the pendency of the case. At one time Choate took the FCC chairman to lunch. This incident became so highly publicized during later appeals and court remands that Sterling Quinlan titled a book he wrote about the case *The Hundred-Million Dollar Lunch,* reflecting the belief that the luncheon contact was instrumental in costing the *Herald-Traveler* a TV license of that value.

The fact that emerges most clearly from a review of the

preceding pages and others to follow in Chapter 7 is that for many years of their existence, the FCC and the FRC ignored or distorted the meaning of the statutes and their own rules and policies in order to justify awarding licenses to politically favored applicants. The investigatory efforts of congressional committees and the decisions of the appellate courts have from time to time forced the agency to mend its ways, and some outstanding chairmen such as James Lawrence Fly, Newton E. Minow, Dean Burch, and Richard E. Wiley have sought to minimize political considerations in the conduct of the commission's business.

The Don Burden Case

The story behind one of the most inglorious episodes in the history of the Federal Communications Commission has never before been told. Participants in the case included a U.S. senator, the head of a federal agency, and the former governor of American Samoa. At the center of it all was an alley fighter named Don W. Burden, who held FCC licenses to operate five broadcasting stations.

Burden gave free political time to Senator Vance Hartke of Indiana during the senator's 1964 campaign for reelection in return for the anticipated intercession of Hartke with the FCC on behalf of Burden's Indianapolis stations. Burden took ten thousand dollars in cash to Portland, Oregon, in what the FCC later declared was a scheme to bribe zoning board members. Burden did a lot of other things that he would have gotten away with had not some of his former employees blown the whistle on him.

Burden first ran afoul of the FCC in 1963 when the commission fined him two thousand dollars for using deceptive station identification announcements on his Vancouver, Washington, station.[31] But most of his troubles stemmed from the way he ran his Indianapolis stations, WIFE-AM and WIFE-FM, as revealed to the commission in complaints it received. Burden bought the stations late in 1963. Two months later he began "hypoing" audience ratings in order to mislead potential advertisers.

"Hypoing" a station's ratings can be done in many ways. One is to launch a major contest in which large sums are given to the audience just before an audience survey is made, thus temporarily enlarging the audience during the rating period. Ten days before a survey was to start, WIFE began a contest offering $113,000 to listeners. Then he persuaded the C. E. Hooper audience survey agency to give WIFE "preliminary" results based on less than two days of audience sampling. He released these figures without revealing that they represented a fragmentary sample. The commission's investigators later found that advertising agency time buyers in New York and Chicago thought the ratings were based on at least a month of sampling.

In an order released on October 28, 1964, the FCC declared Burden's actions "irresponsible" and contrary to its published policies on the use of audience ratings. It renewed his two Indianapolis licenses for only one year, instead of the customary three, for the purpose of "affording the Commission an early opportunity to re-examine your operations and determine the degree of responsibility which you have exhibited during the year."[32] This probationary license was to run until August 1, 1965.

Before that date arrived the FCC learned that the station was engaging in other misleading or fraudulent practices and on April 28, 1966, it designated Burden's renewal application for a hearing. There was, for example, the Eaton Water Filter Contest.

In order to induce the Eaton Manufacturing Company to buy advertising on WIFE, the station offered, as a bonus, to conduct a contest in which listeners were to guess how many gallons of water could pass through an Eaton Water Filter in one week. Each of the three prizes was to be an Eaton Water Filter. However, not a single entry from the public was received, an embarrassing situation since advertisers and Eaton in particular might get the impression that the station had no listeners. So three winners were created—the wife of a WIFE salesman, a station receptionist, and a station secretary. Although none had entered the contest, each received from the station a water filter and a letter of congratulations that made no reference to employee connections. Copies of these letters were sent to the Eaton Company.

There also was the Mystery Santa Claus Contest in which listeners were to guess the identity of a prominent local person whom WIFE dubbed "the Mystery Santa Claus." Clues to his identity were broadcast daily. Prizes were to be awarded to correct entries in the order that they were received. There were twenty-four principal prizes ranging in value from a new car to a radio.

An FCC hearing examiner later found that the top twenty-four winners were not chosen according to the times their correct entries reached the station but were chosen instead by drawing. Moreover, although all twenty-four prizes had been awarded by December 17, WIFE continued to advertise the contest until December 23, with no hint that the most valuable items were gone.

The FCC hearing examiner also found that the stations had repeatedly defrauded advertisers by issuing "affidavits of performance" that misrepresented how many times announcements had been broadcast and whether they were aired in prime time or in less valuable periods. (The FCC has revoked a number of licenses for fraudulent billing of advertisers.)

The initial decision of Hearing Examiner Thomas H. Donahue was to deny renewal of license to WIFE-AM and FM. The decision was released in December 1967.

The initial decisions of hearing examiners became final unless appealed by either party to the commission itself. Then a considerable period of time usually elapsed after an appeal was filed before the commission got around to issuing a final decision.

Leonard Marks, one of Burden's Washington legal counselors, was a man of some importance. As counsel of the LBJ stations, head of the United States Information Agency (USIA), and longtime supporter of Lyndon Johnson, Marks was in a position to influence the appointment of a new member to the FCC to fill an existing vacancy. One candidate for the job was

H. Rex Lee, who had recently been governor of American Samoa.

Word leaked out that Marks had recommended Lee for the appointment. Lee was, in fact, appointed and sworn into office in October 1968. *Broadcasting,* which had excellent White House sources, reported the appointment on September 16, 1968, and added, "It's understood that a principal supporter of Mr. Lee for the Commissioner's post was U.S. Information Agency chief Leonard Marks."

Marks supplied the new commissioner with a legal assistant to help him write opinions. The assistant was Edwin Spievak, who had been on Marks' legal staff at the USIA and who went back to work for Marks at the Cohn & Marks law firm after Lee resigned from the FCC.

The Burden case ground slowly toward a final decision. Oral argument before the commissioners was held on February 10, 1969, after Rex Lee arrived, thus making him eligible to take part in the final decision. That decision was released on October 3, 1969. Although WIFE already was on a probationary, short-term license, and the examiner had found it guilty of committing several more fraudulent practices during the probationary period, four of the seven commissioners voted to give Burden another short-term renewal on the grounds that he had "minimally met the public interest standard."[33]

Commissioners Robert Bartley, Kenneth Cox, and Nicholas Johnson dissented. The Cox-Johnson dissent was long and bitter. It referred to the majority decision as "utterly fantastic" and asked, "How many chances must we give licensees for fraud and misconduct?" Chairman Rosel Hyde and commissioners Robert E. Lee and James Wadsworth voted for renewal. H. Rex Lee issued what was called a "concurring" statement.

In truth, Rex Lee's vote was the deciding one, and his concurring statement was originally intended to serve as the majority opinion. According to a knowledgeable source within the commission, however, the document was inadequate in its attempt to justify another short-term renewal of WIFE's license, and members of the majority directed Henry Geller, general counsel, to write a more credible justification for the majority vote. Geller did his best, although personally opposed to the decision; but he could not come up with a pro-Burden opinion that made much sense, as the Cox-Johnson dissent so vigorously pointed out.

Commissioners Cox, Johnson, and Bartley were not the only ones outraged by the decision; so were members of the House Commerce Committee and its subcommittee on communications. They launched an investigation.

To understand this case in its entirety, we must now go back to April 1966 when the commission designated Burden's Indianapolis applications for hearing because of suspected fraud. Once the hearing was designated by the commission, the Hearing Division of the Broadcast Bureau took over the case as, in effect, the prosecuting attorneys. Like all trial lawyers, hearing division attorneys try to interview potential witnesses in advance in order to learn what their testimony is likely to be. Therefore, a prehearing investigation is made in each case. Larry Berkow, an attorney in the hearing division, and George Curtis, one of the top investigators in the Complaints and Compliance Division, were sent to Indianapolis and Omaha (headquarters of the Burden stations) to conduct prehearing interviews.

They made some unexpected discoveries. During the interval since the original investigation had been made, Burden had fired Ron Mercer, the manager of WIFE. Burden's personal secretary, Louise Rudol, had quit and so had Dorothy Storz, the treasurer of Star Stations, Inc., which was the corporate licensee of Burden's five stations. Mercer, Rudol, and Storz now revealed a great deal of new information. Some of the information was about Vance Hartke's 1964 campaign for reelection to the Senate.

Mercer later testified that in 1964, when Burden thought he was in danger of losing the WIFE license because of his deceptive use of audience ratings, he had called Mercer and told him that Hartke, a member of the Senate Commerce Committee (which had jurisdiction over the FCC), was willing to intercede with the FCC on Burden's behalf if WIFE would give him free advertising in his reelection campaign and preferential treatment in the station's newscasts. Mercer said Burden instructed him to make out an advertising contract for 310 one-minute political announcements promoting Hartke's campaign at $19 each for a total cost of $5,890. On the same day Mercer received a telephone call from the Ruben Advertising Agency in Indianapolis, which handled Hartke's political advertising, to the effect that the agency knew of Burden's arrangement with Hartke and would produce the political spots.

Although Hartke's other political advertising was bought through the Ruben agency, the contract for the 310 spots was to be signed by someone not connected with the campaign. At Hartke's suggestion, Mercer took the contract to Edward Lewis, a friend of the senator, who signed it. Lewis had no connection with the campaign and was not involved in any other purchases of time. The contract stated that WIFE already had received payment for the spots. In fact, no payment had been made, and the commission's final decision in the case found that Burden never had expected payment. The debt eventually was written off the books by Dorothy Storz at Burden's direction.

The FCC later declared that the gift of free time to Hartke violated Section 610 of the U.S. Criminal Code in that it was a political contribution by a corporation. It also found that Burden had falsely reported to the commission that no free time had been given to candidates during the campaign.

As for the WIFE news programs, the station news director, Bill Donnella, testified that he was directed by Mercer to see that Hartke received frequent favorable mentions. When Donnella objected, Mercer told him that Burden had given the order. Donnella then complained to Burden with no result.

The prehearing interviews with potential witnesses turned up other interesting facts. One was that Burden had used his Vancouver station, KISN, to promote the political chances of Governor Mark Hatfield of Oregon, who was running for the U.S. Senate. Star Stations, Inc., had contributed one thousand dollars to the Hatfield campaign (again in violation of the criminal code), and Burden had assigned a reporter to follow Hatfield around and broadcast daily reports on his campaign appearances. No such coverage was given to Hatfield's opponent, U.S. representative Robert Duncan. The FCC found that Burden also had instructed his staff to favor Hatfield in other ways in newscasts. (No evidence was adduced that Hatfield was a party to these arrangements. Burden may merely have been hoping to curry favor with a future senator by doing him unsolicited favors.)

The commission also found that in his efforts to obtain approval of his plan to move the transmitter of his Vancouver station to a different site on the Portland side of the Columbia River, Burden had decided that making ten thousand dollars in political contributions to members of the Multnomah County Zoning Board might help his cause. Therefore, he directed Dorothy Storz to draw that sum in cash from the Star Stations bank account and send it to him. This she did in March 1966, but before Burden could do anything with the money, the board granted the zoning approval that he sought! The FCC later stated

> In our view the evidence . . . supports conclusions that Don Burden undertook a scheme to influence actions of zoning officials . . . by contributing $10,000 to their campaign funds, and that he took overt steps to complete this scheme, although he did not carry it to completion because of the fortuitous circumstance that favorable action was taken on the request before the contributions were made.[34]

The commission investigators learned of Burden's actions in the Hartke and Hatfield campaigns and his zoning board scheme *after* the commission had ordered a hearing on the previously known grounds—fraudulent contests and billing of advertisers. At this stage of the proceeding, the only legal way in which the Broadcast Bureau could introduce evidence of additional violations was to petition the commission to enlarge the issues in the upcoming hearing. This would make the new charges public including those involving a member of the Senate committee that had jurisdiction over the FCC.

When the new evidence was brought to the attention of James Sheridan, then chief of the Broadcast Bureau, Sheridan decided not to make the charges public at that time by petitioning for enlargement of issues but instead to await the outcome of the hearing on the issues already designated. If the commission took away the Indianapolis licenses on the basis of those charges, he reasoned, Burden would have been punished without the necessity of washing the other dirty linen in public including the politically sensitive matter of Senator Hartke. However, it was understood within the staff that if the commission did not take away the licenses, the Broadcast Bureau then would inform it of the additional evidence. Sheridan instructed the two investigators who had conducted the prehearing inquiry to turn over to him their notes and reports for safekeeping in the safe in the bureau chief's office.

Thus matters stood when the commission released its 1969 decision to give Burden another short-term renewal. Soon after the decision was issued, the deputy chief of the Broadcast Bureau, James Juntilla, asked me, since I was chief of the Complaints and Compliance Division, whether a new document was being prepared to inform the commission what the prehearing inquiry had revealed. I had not yet started to do this because the decision would not become final for thirty days, and pending that time nothing could be submitted to the commission about the case under ex parte rules. Juntilla then told me to get the item ready now to present at the end of thirty days, since the House subcommittee had demanded all of our files on Burden and his stations and unless the case was written up quickly, they'd have seized the documents I needed to consult.

I began at once to write a report to the commission on the new evidence. The document also summarized Burden's earlier misdeeds and ended with the recommendation that all of his stations be thrown into hearing. However, there was a major snag. Sheridan had put the material on the prehearing inquiry in his office safe. By this time Sheridan no longer was chief of the Broadcast Bureau. He had been assigned to a task force investigating the role of conglomerates in broadcasting.

Juntilla and I searched the safe and the files in the offices of the bureau chief but found nothing about the Burden case. When we sought out Sheridan, he said he had no recollection of the files, but that if he had brought any to his new office, they would be in the cardboard transfer cases in the corner. A search of the transfer cases revealed nothing relevant.

Fortunately I found that Thomas Fitzpatrick, then chief of the hearing division, still had some of Larry Berkow's material on the prehearing inquiry. Sheridan had not requested Fitzpatrick to turn these papers over to him, apparently because he didn't realize that Fitzpatrick had any.

The mysterious disappearance of the documents raised further congressional suspicions about the Burden case. The House committee called FCC staff members to a closed hearing at which they were questioned individually about the matter.

The FCC itself, which had just acquired a new chairman, Dean Burch, also questioned members of the staff at length, but to the best of my knowledge it never learned what had happened to the missing documents. After reading the new report on the case, however, Chairman Burch suggested that the commission institute a formal inquiry based on the newly revealed evidence. This inquiry verified what Curtis and Berkow had discovered in their prehearing investigation, and the commission then designated all five Burden station licenses for renewal hearing.

Although Burden tried to intimidate his ex-employees Rudol and Storz, they gave full evidence at the hearing, and in a historic decision released on February 7, 1975, the commission took away all five Burden licenses. The decision said

In view of the pervasive and continuing misconduct demonstrated in Burden's operation of his stations, it is clear that Star and Burden lack the requisite qualifications to be licensees of this Commission and that the evidence of record requires the denial of each of Star's renewal applications in this proceeding.[35]

Thus, with imposition of this severest of all sanctions did the commission atone for its previous decision. It should be noted, however, that the final decision followed two significant events: (1) Dean Burch, who believed in enforcing the law, had become chairman; and (2) the House Commerce Committee launched an investigation into the FCC's handling of the case.

There are two interesting footnotes to the story of the Burden case.

1. H. Rex Lee resigned from the commission on December 14, 1973, after the final hearing had been completed but before the commission voted to deny renewal to the Burden stations.

2. In December 1969, more than five years after the end of the 1964 campaign, Senator Hartke's office requested WIFE to send it a bill for the spots it had broadcast. This was shortly after the House Commerce Committee (and doubtless other members of Congress) learned what Curtis and Berkow had discovered about Hartke during their prehearing inquiry. By the time the request for the bill was received, WIFE's records for the 1964 period were incomplete and it could verify only that $3,265 worth of spots had been broadcast. In May 1970 Hartke paid WIFE this amount.

The Five Million Dollar Steal

One of the most unusual stories of political clout, and one never before published, might be called the Five Million Dollar Steal. It goes back to the days of the Federal Radio Commission during the Herbert Hoover administration and requires some explanation because it would not be readily apparent how a Wisconsin governor's campaign for renomination in 1930 could enable a pair of Chicago radio wheeler-dealers to purloin a license for an Indiana station that they would sell years later for more than five million dollars, a record price at the time.

The Wisconsin governor was Walter Kohler, head of the Kohler Company, manufacturer of plumbing equipment. He was a conservative Republican whose term was to expire early in 1931. His opponent for nomination in the September 1930 Republican primary was Philip F. LaFollette, head of the liberal wing of the party in the state and son of former U.S. Senator Robert M. LaFollette, who had run for the presidency on the Progressive party ticket in 1924.

As the GOP primary neared, Kohler began to worry about the outcome and especially about the fact that WIBA, the only radio station in the state capital, Madison, was owned by the liberal *Capital Times,* a staunch supporter of LaFollette. Like its newspaper owner, WIBA was boosting LaFollette's candidacy. The rival *Wisconsin State Journal* backed Kohler, but it had no radio station. In an effort to remedy this situation, the *State Journal* bought a low-power, daytime-only station from Beloit College. The station was moved to Madison and its call letters changed to WISJ ("Wisconsin State Journal").

Next the *State Journal* asked permission from the Republican-dominated Federal Radio Commission to switch its frequency to 780 kilocycles, a much better wavelength, and to use greater power and operate full-time like WIBA. This application was filed only five weeks before the approaching Republican primary of September 16. The radio commission granted it at once.[36] Philip LaFollette, who also was attorney for the *Capital Times,* filed a protest. The chairman of the FRC, Gen. Charles McK. Saltzman, replied that the grant to WISJ to broadcast on 780 kilocycles was only "experimental" and had been made in order to learn whether it would cause any "undue interference" to other stations.

According to those with personal knowledge of the case, the *State Journal* and Kohler had appealed privately to Saltzman to help them offset the damage WIBA was doing to Kohler in the primary campaign. Saltzman agreed to the grant on a temporary basis. In an attempt to conceal the violation of its regulations, the radio commission carried the station on its records as "experimental." However, all other experimental stations listed in the FRC's annual reports to Congress had been assigned call letters that included a numeral such as W8XEN, whereas WISJ's call sign did not.

Even with expedited FRC action, WISJ did not start operating on its new frequency and power until eight days before the primary. Its new frequency was the same as that of Station WMC in Memphis, Tennessee, and only ten kilocycles away from WBBM, a 25,000-watt station in Chicago that was near enough to Madison for WBBM to encounter interference from the new station. WMC and WBBM promptly filed protests with the FRC against the use of the 780-kilocycle frequency by WISJ.

WBBM was owned by the Atlass brothers, H. Leslie and Ralph L., who apparently didn't learn that a Madison station only ten kilocycles away from WBBM had been authorized until their listeners in the Madison area began complaining that WISJ was drowning out the Chicago Cubs baseball broadcasts on WBBM.

The Atlasses petitioned the Supreme Court of the District of Columbia to forbid the FRC to allow WISJ to broadcast on 780 kilocycles. The bill of complaint cited many reasons why the FRC's action had violated its own rules and policies.[37] The court ordered the commission not to issue a regular license to WISJ, but it allowed the station to remain on the air on 780 until a full hearing could be held. The case continued in court until October 11, 1930. Then, without explanation, the Atlass brothers asked dismissal of their complaint, leaving WISJ free to broadcast on 780 kilocycles.

According to my source, the abrupt withdrawal of the Atlass suit came after a little chat that Chairman Saltzman had with the brothers, assuring them that WISJ's use of 780 kilocycles was only temporary and that as soon as an FRC hearing could be held, WISJ would be ordered off the air unless it switched frequencies again. Meanwhile, if the Atlass brothers would kindly stop rocking the boat, the commission would find an appropriate way to reward them later for their understanding attitude. (It should be noted that Kohler himself no longer needed the political support of WISJ after September 16 because LaFollette beat him in the primary.)

The rest of the history of WISJ is short. The FRC held a hearing on the case early in 1931 and the hearing examiner recommended that WISJ's permission to use the new wavelength be terminated because the grant had violated the FRC's own rules. In June 1931 WISJ was "consolidated" (to use the commission's term) with its old rival, WIBA, which still was owned by the *Capital Times*. The WISJ call letters were stricken from the commission's records and the station ceased to exist.[38]

But the Federal Radio Commission's obligation to "do something" for the Atlass brothers had not ended, and they soon took advantage of it. The scene now shifts to Gary, Indiana. At that time Gary had one radio station, WJKS, which was licensed to the Johnson Kennedy Radio Corporation, owned by Thomas J. Johnson and his wife, Frances Kennedy Johnson. The WJKS license required the station to share time with a Chicago station on 1360 kilocycles. This frequency was vastly inferior in coverage potential to the one WJKS soon applied for—560 kilocycles—but 560 already was occupied by two Chicago stations, WIBO and WPCC, which shared time on the air. WIBO was owned by the Nelson Brothers Bond & Mortgage Company. WPCC was owned by the North Shore Church of Chicago, whose share of the time division was twelve hours a week, which it used for religious programming. Whereas Johnson of WJKS later testified that his station always had lost money, WIBO was making a good deal of money. The Nelson brothers had invested $347,000 in WIBO and if its earnings were capitalized on a seven to one ratio, its value was between $500,000 and $700,000.

Thus, there would seem to be a good deal of economic motivation for WJKS to seek the WIBO-WPCC frequency, but a desire for profit was not what the owners of WJKS pleaded when they filed an application on February 16, 1931, for WJKS to move to 560 kilocycles and broadcast full time. They said they merely wanted to provide full-time radio service to the poor foreign-born steel workers, and the schools, churches, and charitable organizations of Gary.

Since assignment of the 560 frequency to a Gary station would cause intolerable interference to any station on that frequency in nearby Chicago, the WJKS application normally would have been rejected forthwith. However, Ralph Atlass had become half owner of WJKS shortly before it filed its application to change wavelengths. A Gary station on 1360 kilocycles, which could broadcast only part time would normally have been of little interest to an experienced Chicago station operator like Ralph Atlass—that is, unless the FRC would grant it full-time operation and a better wavelength. One frequency Ralph seemed to think valuable was 560 kilocycles. In uncontradicted testimony during the later hearing on this case, Alvin Nelson stated that the Atlass brothers had been trying to buy or lease WIBO since 1929 and that in 1930 Ralph had offered to take over operation of the station, pay all expenses, and give the Nelsons one-third of the profits—an offer that they had rejected.[39]

Shortly after Ralph Atlass bought half of WJKS it filed an application to go full time on 560 for two ostensible reasons:

1. WJKS could not provide adequate service to the foreign-born steel workers in Gary or its schools, churches, and charities unless it were allowed to operate full time on 560, which would result in less interference to WJKS from the signals of other stations. Full-time broadcasting was especially important because the steel mills ran twenty-four hours a day, the steel workers worked eight-hour shifts, and many of them could not hear the station at all on its present part-time schedule.

2. Under the terms of the so-called Davis amendment to the Radio Act of 1927, Indiana was an "under-quota" state and Illinois was "over quota" in number and power of broadcasting stations. This imbalance would be partially corrected if WIBO and WPCC were thrown off the air and WJKS were given their frequency, power, and operating schedule. (The Davis amendment did not, in fact, require that each *state* have equal broadcasting facilities. It required that approximately equal facilities be assigned to each of the five *zones* into which the 1927 Radio Act divided the United States for purposes of radio regulation. However, Illinois and Indiana were in the same zone, so by no stretch of the imagination could the law be interpreted to dictate equality of broadcasting facilities between the two states.)

The radio commission ordered a hearing on the WJKS application. It began on April 13, 1931, and continued for seven days. Chief counsel for WJKS was Mabel Walker Willebrandt, who had been an assistant U.S. attorney general under Presidents Harding and Coolidge. This may have been the first but certainly was not to be the last case in which one or both competing parties were represented by attorneys presumed to have political influence with the FRC or FCC.

At the hearing Johnson, president of WJKS, said he always had lost money on the station and that his only object was to serve Gary — especially the foreign-born steel workers. In answer to a direct question from the hearing examiner as to whether he wanted to serve anybody outside the state of Indiana, Johnson replied: "No, sir. We want to serve this local population, serving our community down here. Chicago has enough service of their own. We want to serve our own area."[40]

Atlass also testified that *his* sole intention was to serve

Gary. If allowed to broadcast twenty-four hours a day, he said, WJKS could provide three times as many public service programs geared to the needs of Gary as it now could.

On July 28, 1931, the chief hearing examiner issued an initial decision finding that (1) Gary already was being served adequately by radio stations; (2) WJKS had failed to prove it would suffer less interference on 560 than on its present 1360; (3) WIBO and WPCC were "meritorious stations, serving the public interest, convenience and necessity," and "clear and sound reasons of public policy demand that these broadcasting privileges not be taken from them." Also, there was nothing in the Radio Act, the Davis amendment, or the commission's own rules that would justify granting the WJKS application.

Mabel Walker Willebrandt filed exceptions to the examiner's decision, a normal legal maneuver under the circumstances, and requested oral argument before the commission on the case. Although her actions were normal, the commission's response was not. Instead of calling for reply pleadings from WIBO and WPCC and hearing oral argument on the case, the commission on October 31, 1931, suddenly granted the application of WJKS for 560 kilocycles full time and ordered the secretary of the commission to cancel the WIBO and WPCC licenses within twenty days![41]

In reporting the case, *Broadcasting* magazine stated that the Indiana congressional delegation had "consulted" the FRC on behalf of WJKS.[42]

An indictment of the commission's actions in such cases was made by the Standing Committee on Communications of the American Bar Association.[43] Its report stated, in part,

Formal regulations are strictly enforced in some cases and completely ignored in others . . . literally hundreds of applications have been denied . . . because of alleged violations of the Davis Amendment . . . while during the same period applications have been granted, frequently without hearing, for substantial additional facilities in over-quota states in over-quota zones. In an outstanding example of this sort, two established stations with substantial investments were put out of existence solely because they were located in an over-quota zone, while, during the same period, additional facilities were given without hearing to two other stations in the same city. . . . Violations of identical regulations are considered ground for deleting a station in one case and are not considered sufficient reason even for subjecting another station's renewal application for hearing.

(As will be noted later, subsequent actions by WJKS made even more obvious the seeming hypocrisy of the radio commission and the owners of WJKS.)

WIBO and WPCC appealed the commission's decision, but although the circuit court of appeals reversed it, the U.S. Supreme Court affirmed the decision.[44]

WIBO made one more effort to survive. In May 1933 it petitioned the commission to reopen the case, charging fraud on the part of Ralph Atlass. Although he had testified that the purpose of the WJKS application was to provide better service to Gary, the station had on April 18, 1933, applied to the FRC for authority to move its transmitter from Gary to Hammond, Indiana, which was near the Illinois border and fourteen miles closer to downtown Chicago than the existing WJKS location. It was even three miles closer to the Chicago Loop than was the transmitter of WIBO! The WIBO petition termed Atlass a "professional speculator in broadcasting stations and wavelengths" and asserted that he had recently bought control of WJJD, another Chicago-area station, and was now managing both WJJD and WJKS from the same office and studios in Chicago. WJKS was operating as a Chicago station rather than a Gary one and soliciting advertising from Chicago businesses.

As might be expected in light of the real reasons behind the FRC's decision, it turned down the WIBO petition. Having lost their last appeal, WIBO and WPCC went off the air on June 11, 1933, and WJKS began full-time operation on 560 kilocycles under the new call letters of WIND.

Thereafter the transformation of WIND from a station serving Gary to a full-fledged Chicago outlet proceeded apace. The station obtained authority to increase its daytime power. In reporting to the commission on the station's construction of its new antenna, the Broadcast Engineering Section of the Federal Communications Commission (which by now had replaced the old Federal Radio Commission) stated that WIND had installed a directional antenna that apparently aimed its maximum signal towards Chicago. The chief engineer added, however, that there appeared to be no FCC rule or regulation to prevent this. Although the general counsel of the commission expressed some concern over the directional antenna in view of the prior representations about serving only Gary, the commission made no move to compel the station to live up to its promises.

An application filed by the station in 1939 revealed that the stock ownership of the Johnson family, the original owners, had shrunk from the 50 percent they claimed to have retained after selling stock to Ralph Atlass in 1931 to less than 1 percent. The commission's records do not reveal how much the Johnsons ever got for their stock, but one fact was clear. This small station, once devoted to serving the people of Gary, had now become a powerful Chicago outlet that made no pretense of serving Gary. It even had moved its main studios to Chicago.

And what was the ultimate result of the radio commission's illegal grant of a new frequency to WISJ to help the political ambitions of Walter Kohler? WIND was sold to the Westinghouse Electric Corporation in 1956 for a then all-time record price for a radio station: $5,300,000.

3

The FCC v. Obscene/Indecent Language

Nothing in this Act shall be understood or construed to give the Commission the power of censorship over radio communications or signals transmitted by any radio station, and no regulation or condition shall be promulgated or fixed by the Commission which shall interfere with the right of free speech by means of radio communication.

—Section 326, Communications Act of 1934

Whoever utters any obscene, indecent or profane language by means of radio communication shall be fined not more than $10,000 or imprisoned not more than two years, or both.

—Section 1464, Title 18, U.S. Code

The Commission may revoke any station license or construction permit . . . for violation of section . . . 1464 of title 18 of the United States Code.

—Section 312(a), Communications Act of 1934

But I know it when I see it.

—U.S. SUPREME COURT JUSTICE POTTER STEWART
(after stating that he could not define obscenity)

These quotations may give some idea of the problems the Federal Communications Commission has faced in trying to deal with broadcasts of what it believed to be obscene or indecent language. The courts themselves have had endless difficulties in trying to decide what language is actionable, ever since the first reported American case of this kind, which involved a picture, was decided in Pennsylvania in 1815.[1]

Since we are dealing with broadcasting, we need to consider only the comparatively recent court decisions that have controlled the FCC's major rulings in this area. The first was the Roth case,[2] in which the United States Supreme Court in 1957 adopted this test for obscenity: "Whether, to the average person, applying contemporary community standards, the dominant theme of the material taken as a whole appeals to the prurient interest."[3]

The second was *Memoirs* v. *Massachusetts*,[4] in which the Court in 1966 added the requirement that to be obscene the material must be "utterly without redeeming social value." The Memoirs test had three elements:

(a) The dominant theme of the material taken as a whole appeals to the prurient interest in sex;
(b) The material is patently offensive because it affronts contemporary community standards relating to the description or representation of sexual matters; and
(c) The material is utterly without redeeming social value.[5]

The third case was decided in 1973 and remains the Court's current definition of obscenity. It was *Miller* v. *California*,[6] which amended the Memoirs standard. The Miller test is

(a) Whether the average person, applying contemporary community standards, would find that the work, taken as a whole, appeals to the prurient interest . . .
(b) Whether the work depicts or describes, in a patently offensive way, sexual conduct specifically defined by applicable state law; and,
(c) Whether the work, taken as a whole, lacks serious literary, artistic, political, or scientific value.[7]

The FCC's primary problem for years was to obtain rulings from the courts on whether stricter standards apply to language or pictures when broadcast than to material that is printed or presented in theatrical motion pictures. May language be obscene or indecent when broadcast, even though it does not meet the Roth, Memoirs, or Miller standards? May language be indecent, even though not obscene? It was not until the late 1970s that the commission managed to get both questions answered.

The first recorded effort of the U.S. government to control language used over the air occurred in 1916. The Radio Law of 1912, enacted to regulate dot-and-dash wireless transmission, made no reference to obscene or indecent language. This did not deter the secretary of commerce, who regulated wireless under that law. He issued a "regulation" banning the transmission of "profane or obscene words or language." The Commerce Department's *Radio Service Bulletin* of April 1, 1916, reported that the license of an amateur operator in Stoneham, Massachusetts, had been suspended for three months for use of "profane and abusive language in transmitting messages."

The Radio Act of 1927 contained a section prohibiting the broadcast of "obscene, indecent, or profane language."[8] This was taken over into the Communications Act of 1934 as Section 326. In 1948 it was transferred to the Criminal Code,[9] and the Communications Act was amended to authorize the FCC to revoke licenses for violation of it.[10]

The old Federal Radio Commission denied renewal of the license of KVEP, Portland, Oregon, in 1930 for broadcasting speeches by a political candidate named Robert Gordon Duncan that were held to be obscene, indecent, and/or profane.[11] Duncan himself was fined five hundred dollars on criminal charges and sentenced to six months in prison. In affirming the conviction, the U.S. Court of Appeals for the Ninth Circuit indicated that his violation was in uttering profane rather than obscene language, in that Duncan used "by God" and "damn" irreverently and announced his intention of calling down the curse of God upon certain persons.[12]

There have been few efforts since then to enforce the anti-profanity part of the law. The courts have held that the term does not apply to mere casual use of "hell," "damn," or even "God damn." The Supreme Court indicated support for this attitude in 1952 when it found a law unconstitutional that authorized a censorship board to prohibit exhibition of movies that were "sacrilegious." The Court said, "It is not the business of government in our nation to suppress real or imagined attacks upon a particular religious doctrine."[13]

Flushing Toilets in Denver

Almost thirty years after the Duncan case, the FCC started action against a Denver station for broadcasting "objectionable, off-color and offensive" language, but it blurred the grounds for its action by the use of generalities about the station's failure to serve the public interest, rather than making a clear-cut charge of obscenity.

In 1959 the commission sent KIMN, Denver, an order to show cause why its license should not be revoked because of the language that one or more of its announcers had been using. The examples cited in the document would not qualify as obscene or indecent under present Supreme Court standards.

Here are two examples cited by the FCC in the case:

A card from a listener stating that she took KIMN radio with her wherever she went occasioned this remark [by the station announcer]: "I wonder where she puts KIMN radio when she takes a bath. I may peek. Watch yourself, Charlotte!"

In one instance the announcer remarked: "Say, did you hear about the guy who goosed the ghost, and got a handful of sheet?"[14]

The commission also said the announcer frequently used the sound effect of a toilet being flushed.

On the basis of these and other crude attempts at humor, the FCC began revocation proceedings against the station, which was owned by Cecil L. Heftel (later a congressman from Hawaii and the owner of a station there).

Heftel filed a plea for reconsideration, indicating that he would not contest an order to cease and desist from the objectionable practices if such an order were substituted for the revocation action. Heftel said he had fired the guilty announcer. The FCC remarked that the fact that the material of which Heftel now said he disapproved could have been broadcast for several weeks "indicates a serious laxity in licensee supervision." It decided, nevertheless, merely to order the station to cease such practices rather than to revoke its license. The FCC said, "The Commission, however, is of the view that the remarks in issue, and the respondent's conduct with respect thereto, do not serve the public interest, convenience and necessity, as specifically required by the terms of its license."[15]

Thus, the FCC shied away from basing its case on obscenity-indecency grounds and retreated to the more generalized (and therefore largely unenforceable) standard of "the public interest, convenience and necessity."

Charlie Walker and His Barnyard Humor

What has usually been called "The Charlie Walker Case," because of the name of the offending announcer, ended in 1962 when the FCC refused license renewal to the Palmetto Broadcasting Company, licensee of WDKD, Kingstree, South Carolina.[16] The case became a landmark of sorts because the commission actually took the station off the air rather than backing down as it had with KIMN. When its Palmetto decision was appealed, however, the commission, fearing that it might lose in the higher courts on obscenity-indecency grounds, based its case largely on the fact that the owner of WDKD had not kept control of the station's programming and that he had lied in his testimony during the hearing. The licensee clearly was guilty of both charges, and either was sufficient to cost him his license.

Even though the case cannot be considered an FCC precedent under Section 1464, the Department of Justice later obtained a criminal conviction of Walker personally for violating that statute. The district judge gave Walker a suspended sentence.

The commission's findings against the owner of WDKD, E. G. Robinson, Jr., were fourfold: (1) he had lied to the commission; (2) he had not exercised "appropriate control" over WDKD programming; (3) he had permitted "coarse, vulgar, suggestive material susceptible of indecent double meaning" to be broadcast by Walker; and (4) the station's overall programming did not meet community needs. The FCC noted that Walker had been broadcasting over the station four hours a day for nine years and concluded that "such a pattern of operation is inconsistent with the public interest and cannot remotely be found to be consistent with the licensee's obligation to serve the needs and interests of his area."

Thus, the commission was unwilling to risk a Supreme Court test of whether the objectionable language violated the obscenity statute under the then prevailing standard of the 1957 Roth decision. The test for obscenity adopted by the Supreme Court in that case was "whether, to the average person, applying contemporary community standards, the dominant theme of the material taken as a whole appeals to the prurient interest."

Charlie Walker's barnyard jokes certainly were, as the commission said, "coarse, vulgar, suggestive" and "susceptible of indecent double meaning." The presiding hearing examiner in the case, Thomas Donahue, found that under the Roth test, the broadcasts also were obscene and indecent. Foreshadowing the FCC's ruling many years later in the Pacifica case, Donahue stated that because of the special nature of radio, broadcast matter need not meet the standards for obscenity laid down in Roth before the commission could take action.

The Commission Defines "Indecent" Language

After beating around the bush in the KIMN and WDKD cases the commission finally made an attempt to define indecent language in a case that arose in 1970.[17]

WUHY-FM, a noncommercial, educational station in Philadelphia, broadcast a prerecorded interview at 10 P.M. with Jerry Garcia, leader of the rock group The Grateful Dead. Garcia expressed his views on ecology, music, philosophy, and other subjects. It wasn't his subject matter that the FCC was concerned about. It was the fact that almost every sentence contained gratuitously inserted words such as "fuck" and "shit" or variations thereof. The notice of liability for forfeiture that the commission sent to the station contained the following examples:

S..t, man.
I must answer the phone 900 f....n' times a day, man.
This kind of s..t.
It's f....n' rotten, man. Every f....n' year.
Political change is so f.....g slow.

The commission said it had a duty to act to prevent the widespread use on broadcast outlets of such expressions in these circumstances.

The speech involved has no redeeming social value and is patently offensive by contemporary community standards . . . it conveys no thought to begin some speech with "s..t" or to use "f.....g" as an adjective throughout the speech . . . its use can be avoided on radio without stifling in the slightest way any thought which the person wishes to convey.[18]

Further, said the FCC,

If WUHY can broadcast an interview with Mr. Garcia where he begins sentences with "S..t, man . . . " or uses "f.....g" before word after word just because he likes to talk that way, so also can any other person on radio. . . . The consequences of any such widespread practice would be to undermine the usefulness of radio to millions of others. For these expressions are patently offensive to millions of listeners. And here it is crucial to bear in mind the difference between radio and other media. Unlike a book, which requires the deliberate act of purchasing and reading (or a motion picture where admission to public exhibition must be actively sought), broadcasting is disseminated generally to the public under circumstances where reception requires no activity of this nature. Thus, it comes directly into the home and frequently without any advance warning of its content. . . . Further, in [the] audience are very large numbers of children. Were this type of programming . . . to become widespread, it would drastically affect the use of radio by millions of people. No one could ever know, in home or car listening, when he or his children would encounter what he would regard as the most vile expressions serving no purpose but to shock, to pander to sensationalism.[19]

The FCC acknowledged that the broadcast was not obscene because it did not have "a dominant appeal to prurience or sexual matters," but it said it was indecent under Section 1464 because in the broadcast field the standard for indecency should be that the material "is (a) patently offensive by contemporary community standards; and (b) is utterly without redeeming social value."[20]

The FCC conceded that there was no precedent for this ruling and said the matter was one of first impression, which could be definitely settled only by the courts. In order to make an appeal possible it imposed a nominal forfeiture of one hundred dollars and said it would welcome a court review, which WUHY could obtain by merely refusing to pay the fine.

Perhaps because an appeal would have cost far more in legal fees than one hundred dollars and perhaps because it didn't want further bad publicity that might result from a trial, the station paid the fine, and the FCC was frustrated in its effort to get a judicial definition of "indecent." But at least it had announced its own definition.

The FCC Puts an End to "Topless Radio"

In their scramble to attract larger audiences, some radio stations in the early 1970s began devoting their traditional housewives' "open mike" or "call-in" shows to explicit discussions of sex. Within the broadcasting world these programs became known as "topless radio." They did attract larger audiences, usually in proportion to the brashness of the announcers conducting them and the willingness of some female callers to engage in explicit descriptions of their own sexual activities.

Complaints soon began to arrive at the FCC, and rumblings were heard from Congress. As chief of the commission's Complaints and Compliance Division, I decided to try to learn how widespread the practice was and whether the language broadcast actually violated Section 1464. I requested the regional offices of the commission's Field Operations Bureau to tape-record the programs in their cities that generated the most local complaints and to forward the tapes to Washington.

Sixty-one hours of tapes were received. Attorneys were assigned to review the tapes and to excerpt the portions that they thought might violate Section 1464. The final, edited version for presentation to the commission contained twenty-two minutes of excerpts from several stations. Chairman Dean Burch called a closed meeting in his office on March 21, 1973, at which the commissioners heard the tape—that is, all but Commissioner Nicholas Johnson, the commission's ultraliberal, who refused to take part other than to stick his head in the door long enough to denounce the entire proceeding as contrary to the First Amendment.

After hearing the tape, the commissioners authorized the staff to draw up a notice of apparent liability for forfeiture to be sent to WGLD-FM, Oak Park, Illinois, which seemed to be by far the worst offender, and voted to hold a formal inquiry into the whole subject. Additionally, Chairman Burch told the other commissioners that in his address to the upcoming annual convention of the National Association of Broadcasters (NAB) he was going to urge broadcasters to exercise self-restraint in this area in order to avoid possible action against them by the commission, Congress, and the courts. On the day before Burch gave this speech, the National Association of Broadcasters, itself concerned about the growing trend among some member stations, adopted a resolution condemning sexually oriented call-in shows. (The FCC inquiry later was canceled.)

The four-way combination of the forfeiture action against WGLD, the announcement of a formal FCC inquiry into the subject, Burch's speech to the NAB convention, and the NAB's own resolution had the intended result. Topless radio shows disappeared from the airwaves, but all obscene or indecent broadcasts did not, as will be seen.

In the WGLD case, the commission held for the first time that the material broadcast was obscene under the Supreme Court's definition of that term. It also found that the language met its test for indecency as set forth in the WUHY decision.[21]

The WGLD program was titled "Femme Forum" and was broadcast five days a week from 10 A.M. to 3 P.M. The passages from the program cited in the FCC's Notice of Apparent Liability contained language far different from that usually used in a government document, but the commission saw no other way to demonstrate the basis for its ruling.

On February 23, 1973, the topic was "oral sex." The program consisted of very explicit exchanges in which the female callers spoke of their oral sex experiences. One such passage was as follows:

Female Listener: . . . of course, I had a few hangups at first about — in regard to this, but you know what we did — I have a craving for peanut butter all that time so I used to spread this on my husband's privates and after awhile, I mean, I didn't even need the peanut butter any more.
Announcer: (Laughs) Peanut butter, huh?
Listener: Right. Oh, we can try anything, you know — any, any of these women that have called and they have, you know, hangups about this — I mean they should try their favorite — you know, like, uh . . .
Announcer: Whipped cream, marshmallow . . .
Listener: You know, I mean, it's a little messy but outside of that it's great . . .

Several callers referred to the "hangup" of avoiding having the husband climax "when I go down on him. . . . " Another caller stated that " . . . initially what I was afraid of was the climaxing end of it. I thought I'd choke to death, you know, and come to find out, it not only can taste good but it isn't all that much. . . . " Still another referred to a "hangup" of her husband that " . . . he was afraid I was gonna bite it off." A caller on the February 21 program on "How do you keep your sex life alive?" said that "when you make oral love to the man, have a mouth full of hot water — that really turns him on." Another exchange on the February 21 broadcast was as follows:

Announcer: O.K. Jennifer. How do you keep your sex life alive?
Listener: Well, actually, I think it's pretty important to keep yourself mentally stimulated most of the time and then when you are with that person it's that much better for you.
Announcer: Uh, hum. And how do you do that?
Listener: Oh, you think about how much fun you're going to be having.
Announcer: . . . That's all it takes?
Listener: Well, no. (Laughs)
Announcer: Well, what more does it take?
Listener: Well, there—well—if that doesn't work there are different little things you can do.
Announcer: Like?
Listener: Well, like oral sex when you're driving is a lot of fun. It takes the monotony out of things.
Announcer: I can imagine.
Listener: The only thing is you have to watch out for truck drivers.
Announcer: Uh, hum. O.K., that sounds like good advice.
Listener: Try it sometime. You might like it.
Announcer: Try it—you'll like it! What else, my dear?
Listener: Oh well, that's about enough for right now.[22]

The commission found that under the Roth test and the later *Memoirs* v. *Massachusetts* decision, this sort of language was obscene.

The FCC said programs like "Femme Forum" were "designed to garner large audiences through titillating sexual discussions" and that "the announcer actively solicits the titillating response." Again, the widespread dissemination of radio broadcasts was an important consideration. It continued:

If discussions in this titillating and pandering fashion of coating the penis to facilitate oral sex, swallowing the semen at climax, overcoming fears of the penis being bitten off, etc. do not constitute broadcast obscenity within the meaning of 18 U.S.C. 1464, we do not perceive what does or could. We also believe that the dominant theme here is clearly to appeal to the prurient interest. The announcer coaxed responses that were designed to titillate—to arouse sexual feelings. . . . Indeed, again in this very program one caller stated that as a result of what she had heard on the program, she was going to try oral sex that night. . . . Finally, from what has been discussed, we do not believe that there is redeeming social value here. This is not a serious discussion of sexual matters, but rather titillating, pandering exploitation of sexual materials.

Our conclusions here are based on the pervasive and intrusive nature of broadcast radio, even if children were left completely out of the picture. However, the presence of children in the broadcast audience makes this an *a fortiori* matter. There are significant numbers of children in the audience during these afternoon hours—and not all of pre-school age. Thus, there is always a significant percentage of school-age children out of school on any given day. Many listen to radio; indeed it is almost the constant companion of the teenager.[23]

The commission then cited a call during one program in which a mother protested the broadcast of such material and said her thirteen-year-old daughter happened to be at home that day listening to music on WGLD when "Femme Forum" began.[24]

The FCC found the program to be indecent as well as obscene on the basis of its definition of indecency in the WUHY case. The commission imposed a forfeiture of two thousand dollars on Sonderling Broadcasting Corporation for broadcast of obscene and indecent language, which was the maximum fine possible for two days of violation under the forfeiture statute then in effect. As in the WUHY case, the commission declared that it would welcome an appeal that would open the door to "judicial consideration of our action."

Once again, the licensee refused to go to court. Sonderling protested the "injustice" of the fine but said that because of "the tremendous financial burden" of pursuing the case in the courts, it would pay it.

At the time, Sonderling Broadcasting Corporation was owner of several profitable television and radio stations and easily could have borne the expense of an appeal. Egmont Sonderling, owner of the corporation, perhaps chose not to appeal the case because he was embarrassed by it and wanted it forgotten as soon as possible. It should be said that Sonderling's other stations were operated for years with few if any violations.

Although Sonderling declined to help the FCC obtain a judicial forum on broadcast obscenity, two Chicago organizations did by filing applications for reconsideration of the commission's action. They were the Illinois division of the American Civil Liberties Union and a group named the Illinois Citizens Committee for Broadcasting.

The U.S. Court of Appeals for the District of Columbia Circuit affirmed the FCC's ruling that the broadcasts were obscene.[25] Like most courts, however, it refused to rule on anything more than it had to. It said that, having held that the language violated Section 1464 by being obscene, it need not rule on whether it also was indecent.

As is customary in U.S. circuit courts of appeal, the WGLD case had been considered by a panel of three members of the nine-judge court. The petitioners next asked for a rehearing by the entire court. A majority of the nine judges voted to deny a rehearing, but Judge David Bazelon, an extreme liberal, disagreed. Bazelon was the Nicholas Johnson of the court (he often quoted Johnson's dissenting FCC opinions favorably), and he wrote a long dissent to the decision.

The FCC had at last obtained a federal appellate ruling on obscene language, and when the Supreme Court declined to review the circuit court's decision in 1973, the decision became final.

Obscenity in the Ivy League

Before taking up the final significant case of this kind, we will review briefly one in which the FCC decided to make an example of a university whose student-operated station was broadcasting material even more objectionable than that of the commercial stations.

In its original allocation of FM station channels, the FCC set aside many for noncommercial, educational purposes. Most of these licenses were granted to universities and colleges. Some of the college stations, like WAMU of American University in Washington, D.C., and WOI of Iowa State University in Ames, were operated under the control of the university and provided excellent programming for the public and their students. Others were abandoned by the schools to the unsupervised control of students. They often became playthings of the most irresponsible members of the student body. FCC staff members called them "sand boxes."

Although the commission had received complaints that some college stations were broadcasting obscene language, it did nothing much about them until it was confronted with a particularly offensive example at WXPN(FM), which was licensed to the University of Pennsylvania.

After receiving complaints about the station, the FCC taped a program called "The Vegetable Report" on January 20 and 27, 1975. It was an "open mike," call-in show conducted by three students from 4 to 7 P.M. The language used was nauseating.

Shortly after the commission began its investigation of the case, the trustees and the president of the university — apparently learning for the first time what their station had been broadcasting — began belated efforts at correction. They suspended the so-called constitution of the station, issued a set of programming guidelines, dismissed the three students who conducted "The Vegetable Report" from the staff of the station, and gave authority over WXPN to the director of student activities.

The director already possessed vague authority over the station, and he had long been unhappily aware of what was being broadcast. However, under the university's complex system of "democratic" student government, the director had not been able to do anything about the situation until the FCC investigation jolted the authorities into action.

The commission found that the language broadcast was both obscene and indecent and fined the station two thousand dollars, which was at that time the statutory maximum for two days of violations.[26] The commission also designated the renewal application of WXPN(FM) for hearing on grounds that the university had abandoned control over it, as it obviously had.[27]

The university paid the fine but elected to contest the threat to its license renewal. After a hearing the FCC denied renewal of the license and WXPN went off the air.[28] Later the university filed a new application for the now unoccupied channel. The commission granted the application, satisfied that the school had learned its lesson.

The commission's drastic action against a distinguished Ivy League school was not ignored by other educational institutions with student-operated stations. If they had not already been doing so they began supervising the stations. One, Georgetown University, decided to turn in its license and go off the air. It, too, had been having problems with a volunteer student staff.

George Carlin and the Seven Filthy Words

The FCC had won the Sonderling case on broadcast obscenity, but it had no judicial guidelines on broadcast indecency until the Pacifica Foundation case was decided by the U.S. Supreme Court in 1978.[29]

Ironically, there was a major argument within the commission itself on whether to appeal this case to the Supreme Court after the D.C. Circuit Court of Appeals had reversed the commission's decision. The FCC had ruled that although the language broadcast by Pacifica station WBAI(FM) was not obscene, it was indecent.

The FCC does not like to appeal cases to the Supreme Court unless the Department of Justice joins in the appeal. The Court is less likely to view an appeal by a government agency with favor if the Department of Justice refuses to join in it, because that department is supposed to prosecute such appeals on behalf of the federal government. In the Pacifica case, the Justice Department was most reluctant. Like some FCC commissioners and some members of the general counsel's staff, the department feared the Court would rule against the commission. Other members of the FCC staff, including General Counsel Ashton Hardy and me, believed the Court would affirm the commission's ruling and that, in any event, there was never likely to be a stronger case for the proposition that certain broadcast language, although not obscene, could be indecent under Section 1464. Chairman Richard E. Wiley and a majority of the commissioners voted in favor of an appeal, but the Justice Department refused to join in the action.

WBAI(FM), located in New York City, and the five other stations licensed to the nonprofit Pacifica Foundation have been the subjects of many complaints to the FCC over the years because of their unusual programming. They aroused strong feelings. When Pacifica opened a station in Houston, Texas, someone twice bombed its antenna tower to the ground. Undaunted, Pacifica rebuilt the tower and continued spreading its social, economic, and political philosophy.

The WBAI case began when the FCC received a complaint that in the early afternoon of October 30, 1973, while driving in his car with his young son, the complainant heard a WBAI broadcast using the words "cocksucker," "cunt," and "shit." WBAI's response to this statement was that it had been playing a record by comedian George Carlin as part of a program about contemporary society's attitudes toward language. Immediately before the broadcast of Carlin's nightclub monologue, listeners had been told that it contained language "which might be regarded as offensive to some." Pacifica asserted that Carlin was "a significant social satirist of American manners and language in the tradition of Mark Twain and Mort Sahl."

Carlin's comedy monologue, as quoted in full in the FCC ruling and the Supreme Court decision, was delivered before a nightclub audience and dealt with what he called "the seven filthy words" that could not be used on the air. They were "shit, piss, fuck, cunt, cocksucker, motherfucker, and tits."

The Supreme Court's definition of obscene language required that it arouse prurient sexual interest. Carlin's language was not obscene because it was not likely to have that result. Instead, said the commission, the language was indecent because it was broadcast at a time when children might be listening. The FCC said,

We believe that patently offensive language, such as that involved in the Carlin broadcast, should be governed by principles which are analogous to those found in cases relating to public nuisance. . . . Nuisance

law generally speaks to *channeling* behavior more than actually prohibiting it. The law of nuisance does not say, for example, that no one shall maintain a pigsty; it simply says that no one shall maintain a pigsty in an inappropriate place, such as a residential neighborhood. In order to avoid the error of overbreadth, it is important to make it explicit whom we are protecting and from what . . . the most troublesome part of this problem has to do with the exposure of children to language which most parents regard as inappropriate for them to hear.
. . . Therefore, the concept of "indecent" is intimately connected with the exposure of children to language that describes, in terms patently offensive as measured by contemporary community standards for the broadcast medium, sexual or excretory activities and organs, at times of day when there is a reasonable risk that children may be in the audience. Obnoxious, gutter language describing these matters has the effect of debasing and brutalizing human beings by reducing them to their mere bodily functions, and we believe that such words are indecent within the meaning of the statute and have no place on radio when children are in the audience. In our view, indecent language is distinguished from obscene language in that (1) it lacks the element of appeal to the prurient interest . . . and that (2) when children may be in the audience, it cannot be redeemed by a claim that it has literary, artistic, political or scientific value.[30]

Since this was a case of first impression the commission did not threaten to revoke the license or even to impose a fine. Instead it issued a declaratory order defining indecent language for broadcast purposes, in order to "clarify the . . . standards" and to give anyone who considered himself aggrieved by the ruling a chance to seek judicial review. The FCC wanted to let everyone know how it intended to interpret the indecent language part of Section 1464 in the future.

Pacifica appealed the order to the D.C. Circuit Court of Appeals. The court reversed the commission on a two-to-one vote.[31]

The Supreme Court granted certiorari and upheld the commission's ruling, five to four.[32] The majority was composed of Justices Stevens, Rehnquist, Blackmun, and Powell and Chief Justice Burger. (All five did not agree on all parts of Stevens's majority opinion but concurred in the result.) Brennan, Marshall, Stewart, and White dissented. The minority declared that "indecent" had the same meaning as "obscene" and that since Carlin's words were not obscene, they were not indecent, either. The majority held that indecent had a meaning different from obscene and that under the particular circumstances of this case (i.e., time of broadcast when numbers of children were likely to be in the audience), the broadcast language was indecent. The court said that of all forms of communication, broadcasting has received the most limited First Amendment protection because "patently offensive, indecent material presented over the airwaves confronts the citizen, not only in public, but also in the privacy of the home, where the individual's right to be left alone plainly outweighs the First Amendment rights of an intruder." The Court also stated that "broadcasting is uniquely accessible to children, even those too young to read. . . . The ease with which children may obtain access to broadcast material . . . amply justifies special treatment of indecent broadcasting."[33]

Having at last achieved its objective of a Supreme Court definition of indecent language, the FCC proceeded to do nothing during the next nine years to enforce the court-approved standard. Then on April 16, 1987, it came to life, issuing warnings to three stations for broadcast of indecent language and announcing what it called "new standards to clarify its enforcement authority over such broadcasts in the future."[34] (One of the three stations was another Pacifica station, KPFK-FM, Los Angeles.) The most astonishing part of its statement was the admission that for years it had been limiting its definition of indecent language to the specific "seven dirty words" broadcast in the George Carlin monologue. As anyone who read the Pacifica decision knew, the Supreme Court did not restrict its definition to Carlin's so-called seven dirty words or to any other specific language.

This, of course, the commission knew, and acknowledged (in a backhanded fashion) by stating that henceforth it would apply what it chose to term "the *generic* definition of indecency advanced in *Pacifica*," which, it said, was "language or material that depicts or describes, in terms patently offensive as measured by contemporary community standards for the broadcast medium, sexual or excretory activities or organs." The commission candidly added,

In recent years the Commission has interpreted the indecency standard in such a narrow fashion that there have been no findings of violations since the original Pacifica case in 1976. Today, by deciding to apply the broader definition set forth in Pacifica, the Commission demonstrated its commitment to enforce the statutory prohibitions against unlawful obscene or indecent transmissions.

It is, to say the least, highly unusual for a federal agency to admit that it had been ignoring the law as interpreted by the U.S. Supreme Court. Because its "prior rulings may have created uncertainties as to the scope of actionable indecency," it said it was merely issuing warnings to the three licensees.

Another Flip-Flop

The commission maintained its on-again, off-again record for dealing with obscenity and indecency in a still later case involving an application for license renewal of station WSNS-TV (VIDEO 44), Chicago, which was contested by a rival applicant, Monroe Communications Corporation. The FCC's Review Board found evidence that WSNS-TV had broadcast obscene movies[35] and added an issue on that subject to the others in the comparative hearing.

The commission reversed the Review Board and stated that it would take no action in *any* obscenity case *unless the station licensee already had been criminally convicted of violating Section 1464!*[36] It stated,

In formulating its obscenity criteria, the Supreme Court anticipated that determinations would be made by local juries based on their familiarity with local community standards. Obviously, no such mechanism could be applied in Commission proceedings. . . . Accordingly, we believe that it would be desirable to rely on local prosecutors to recognize situations in which a perceived threat to local community standards actually exists.

In this decision the commission ignored the fact that in the Pacifica case the Supreme Court had imposed no such condition when it found Carlin's language indecent, and that no such prerequisite to FCC action was required in the Sonderling obscenity case by either the D.C. Circuit Court of Appeals or the Supreme Court, which denied certiorari.

Monroe Communications petitioned for reconsideration, pointing out that the commission itself had recently taken action under Section 1464 in three indecency cases (noted previously), and that the *Final Report* of the Attorney General's Commission on Pornography specifically recommended that the commission actively enforce antiobscenity laws.

In the face of these arguments the commission backed down by admitting "we are persuaded, on reflection, that we should retain the ability to pursue a range of options when allegations of a violation of section 1464 are raised [including] undertaking our own action and exercising one of the many administrative sanctions available to us."[37]

However, the commission found another reason to avoid the obscenity issue, the timeliness of the complaint.

Allegations that a licensee has broadcast obscene material should be presented to the Commission at the time of the broadcast or soon thereafter. Considering allegations at that time will allow the Commission to take action that will remedy in a timely manner any violation that may be occurring. If no complaints are received until the end of the license term, then the licensee may well continue to air materials that violate the law. On the other hand, if complaints are brought contemporaneously, any adverse action of the Commission will put the licensee on notice that its conduct is unacceptable.

The commission went on to say that the complaints it received at the times of the WSNS-TV broadcasts did not "present the prima facie showing necessary for the Commission to initiate an investigation into a possible obscenity violation." Just what the current FCC would consider to constitute the necessary "prima facie showing" was not clear.

In an effort to learn how many contemporaneous complaints against Station WSNS-TV were received and whether they made a "prima facie showing," I asked to inspect the station's complaint folder on May 4, 1988. I was told that the folder was not in the files and therefore was unavailable for inspection. No reasons were given for its absence.

The claim that receipt of contemporaneous complaints would have enabled the commission to "initiate an investigation" has a hollow ring to persons familiar with current FCC practices. As will be explained further in Chapter 8, the Reagan commission almost never made a field investigation of a complaint. In what seemed to be a search for a way to exclude an obscenity issue in this case, the commission, in effect, established a statute of limitations on broadcast violations even though no criminal prosecution is involved. Under such a policy previous commissions would have been forced to throw out evidence in several major cases. For example, in the Burden case (Chapter 2) the commission received no contemporaneous complaints about Burden's scheme to bribe the Multnomah County Zoning Board or his illegal deal with Senator Hartke. Therefore, it never put him "on notice" that his conduct was "unacceptable." Presumably, the Reagan commission would have thrown out the evidence. It presumably would have done the same in the WOOK case (Chapter 6) where it came to light in another contested renewal proceeding that the station had been broadcasting tips on the numbers game in the guise of citing chapter and verse from the Bible. Here, again, "contemporaneous" complaints never enabled the commission to put the licensee "on notice" that such fraudulent religious programs violated federal statutes.

Thus, the commission's record on enforcing the obscenity-indecency statute is a mixed bag. For many years it sought diligently to obtain the court definitions of these terms that were necessary for enforcement. But having obtained the definitions, it ceased action in this area for many years, principally because the Reagan-appointed commission was opposed to enforcing much of anything. Then, in 1987 it roused itself long enough to send letters of reprimand to three stations but returned to its old ways thereafter by concocting excuses for its failure to act in the WSNS-TV case.

4

The Fairness Doctrine

The *fairness doctrine,* which was created to deal with the broadcast of controversial public issues, itself became one of the most controversial of all FCC policies. Almost sixty years after it was sired by the old Federal Radio Commission, it was slain in 1987 by the Federal Communications Commission with the assistance of Circuit Court of Appeals Judge Robert Bork and President Ronald Reagan. This occurred despite a Supreme Court decision upholding the doctrine and legislation rushed through Congress in 1987 to make it an undeniable part of the Communications Act.

It is probable that the Congress, the courts, or the FCC itself under a different administration will resurrect the doctrine. Let us have a look at this unusual FCC regulation—unusual for the following reasons.

1. Despite its name, it never purported to bring about real fairness in broadcasting public issues.
2. It led to endless breast-beating by some broadcasters, who claimed it violated the First Amendment, although the U.S. Supreme Court voted unanimously that it was constitutional.
3. Despite all of the protesting, no station ever lost its license because of fairness doctrine violations.[1]

4. It was widely misunderstood by members of the public, many of whom thought it guaranteed "equal time."

In simplest terms, the fairness doctrine required broadcast stations to cover important public issues and to try to present contrasting views on these issues. It did not require equal time for opposing points of view. That term applies only to broadcasts by political candidates. In fact, the FCC has ruled that disparities of as great as five to one in amounts of time given to opposing viewpoints might comply with its fairness requirements.

The fairness doctrine did not require that opposing sides of an issue be broadcast on the same program or even the same series of programs, nor did it require the broadcaster to grant reply time to the complainant personally. The broadcaster could choose anyone he or she deemed competent to present the other side.

Moreover, as administered by the FCC, a person who filed a fairness complaint bore a heavy burden in order to bring about even a preliminary inquiry by the FCC into the complaint. First, he or she must have taken the complaint to the station or network. If turned down there, the complaint to the commission must state what network or station broadcast what side of what controversial issue of public importance. The complainant must define the issue specifically and say why it was controversial and of public importance.

Finally, he or she must set forth reasons for believing that the network or station has not broadcast contrasting views on the issue at *any* time.

Offhand, this appeared to raise an insurmountable barrier to the filing of fairness complaints, since it seemed to require that the complainant have tuned in the station for twenty-four hours a day, seven days a week, in order to bolster a claim that the "other side" never was broadcast. However, the commission accepted, as meeting this test, a statement that the complainant normally followed the news and public affairs programs of the station and that, to the best of his or her knowledge, these programs had not presented a contrasting view.[2]

Because of these stringent requirements, the FCC staff rejected the overwhelming majority of fairness complaints with letters explaining why they were faulty. Most often, the complainant had not stated reasons for concluding that the station never presented contrasting views.

The FCC adopted these stringent threshold requirements and otherwise loaded the dice in favor of broadcasters because it did not want to discourage stations from dealing with controversial issues. It sought to minimize the danger that the doctrine would have a "chilling effect" on broadcast journalism as its critics claimed. In the course of their news, commentary, and discussion programs, stations present thousands of views on controversial issues expressed by public officials, spokespersons for special interest groups, members of the public, and their own commentators. If the mere allegation that a station once broadcast only one side of an issue were enough to compel the station to research and reply to a complaint, it might decide to broadcast very little about public issues, and the electorate would be the loser.

How It Began

The principles underlying the fairness doctrine go back to the old Federal Radio Commission in the late 1920s. In the Great Lakes Broadcasting Co. case (see Chapters 1 and 6), the radio commission said

It would not be fair, indeed it would not be good service, to the public to allow a one-sided presentation of the political issues of a campaign. Insofar as a program consists of a discussion of public questions, public interest requires ample play for the free and fair competition of opposing views, and the Commission believes that the principle applies not only to addresses by political candidates but to all discussions of issues of importance to the public.[3]

The Federal Communications Commission reaffirmed these principles and later set forth the fairness doctrine in its 1949

Report on Editorializing by Broadcast Licensees as it thereafter was administered. Here the commission stated (1) a broadcaster has "an affirmative responsibility to provide a reasonable amount of time for the presentation . . . of programs devoted to the discussion and consideration of public issues," and (2) "broadcast licensees have an affirmative duty generally to encourage and implement the broadcast of all sides of controversial public issues . . . over and above their obligation to make available upon demand opportunities for the expression of opposing views."[4]

In its 1974 *Fairness Report* the commission reexamined all aspects of the doctrine, clarified its interpretation, and reaffirmed it. Richard E. Wiley, general counsel of the FCC when this project began and later chairman of the commission, headed the committee that drafted the report. I was a member of it.

Meanwhile, Congress had given what was almost universally understood to be statutory authority to the doctrine. In amending Section 315(a) of the Communications Act in 1959, it affirmed "the obligation imposed upon [broadcasters] under this Act to operate in the public interest and to afford reasonable opportunity for the discussion of conflicting views on issues of public importance."[5]

A Prohibitionist and an Atheist Complain

The FCC did little to enforce the doctrine before 1962 except to issue "pious admonitions," as was noted in the October 1961 issue of the *George Washington University Law Review*. For example, it took no action about two significant cases that arose in 1946, each raising a problem that was to plague it for years to come.

In one case the Reverend Sam Morris, a prohibitionist, petitioned the commission to deny license renewal to Station KRLD, Dallas, Texas, because the station had broadcast CBS programs advertising wine and beer while it and CBS had refused to sell him time in which to counsel "abstinence from the drinking of such alcoholic beverages."

CBS and KRLD replied that the advertising of commercial goods did not raise controversial questions because advertising was not "propaganda." The FCC did not agree. It found that "advertising is, in essence, a form of propaganda" and that, although differences of opinions on the relative merits of one product over another do not ordinarily raise issues of public importance, the advertising of wine and beer could raise such issues, particularly in view of the fact that under local option laws almost half of KRLD's audience lived in dry counties.

However, the commission found a way to duck the issue. It said the problem was industrywide and not restricted solely to KRLD. Therefore, "the petition, involving, as it does, issues of such extensive scope, should not be granted as to one particular station, when there is no urgent ground for selecting it rather than another."[6]

This seems logically equivalent to deciding not to ticket one traffic violator because there are many other traffic violators. It did not appear to occur to the commission to take up the issue on a nationwide basis if the problem was as important as it seemed to think. More likely, this idea did occur to at least some members, but they were not willing to do anything that would make advertising of commercial products subject to fairness doctrine debate. That would come years later when a less cautious commission was to burn its fingers trying to apply the doctrine to cigarette advertising.

Four months after the Morris decision the FCC used the same escape hatch to avoid acting on a complaint filed by an atheist. This was the Scott case, wherein Robert Harold Scott of Palo Alto, California, asked the commission to revoke the licenses of three stations because they had refused to sell or give time to him to espouse the cause of atheism, although they had permitted the use of their facilities "for direct statements and arguments against atheism, as well as for indirect arguments, such as church services, prayers, Bible readings, and other kinds of religious programs." Scott asserted that the question of the existence or nonexistence of a Divine Being was a controversial issue, and that in refusing to make time available for the atheistic point of view, the stations were not presenting all sides of the issue and, therefore, were not operating in the public interest.[7]

This was an even hotter potato than Reverend Morris had tried to hand the FCC, and the canny politicians comprising that body were not about to accept it and incur the possible wrath of God-fearing Americans.

As in the Morris case, the commission agreed with the basic complaint.

Freedom of religious belief necessarily carries with it freedom to disbelieve, and freedom of speech means freedom to express disbeliefs as well as beliefs. If freedom of speech is to have meaning, it cannot be predicated on the mere popularity or public acceptance of the ideas sought to be advanced. It must be extended as readily to ideas which we disapprove or abhor as to ideas which we approved.[8]

The commission waxed eloquent on the subject. To deny atheists the right to expression, it said, might mean that "Jefferson, Jackson, Lincoln and others whose names we revere could, today, be barred from access to the air to express their own particular religious philosophies."

Having embraced the arguments of the complainant, the FCC told him to get lost. It said that "the issue here involved is one of broad scope and is not restricted to the three stations which are the subject of Mr. Scott's complaint. We therefore do not feel that we would be warranted on the basis of this single complaint in selecting these three stations as the subject of a hearing looking toward termination of their licenses."[9]

This was the nearest the FCC ever came to applying the fairness doctrine to matters of religious faith. Madalyn Murray O'Hair and other atheists filed complaints in later years, but all were turned down. Scott, himself, kept filing complaints for the next three decades under the delusion that the commission's language in the 1946 decision presaged favorable action.

Cullman, Red Lion, et al.

The commission worked out its final definition of the fairness doctrine and its policies for enforcing it in a series of leading cases that arose in the 1960s and 1970s.

In the Cullman Broadcasting Co. case in 1963 it ruled that a licensee who sold time for the presentation of one side of an issue could not refuse access to contrasting views merely because nobody wanted to buy time for that purpose. The primary consideration, it said, was the public's right to hear contrasting views on important public issues.[10]

It was this same question on which the FCC's decision turned in the most famed fairness case of all — *Red Lion Broadcasting Co.* v. *FCC* — in which the United States Supreme Court affirmed the constitutionality of the fairness doctrine and the personal attack rule, which the commission had appended to it.[11] The Reverend John M. Norris (a friend and ally of the Reverend Carl McIntire, whose exploits are described in Chapter 6) owned a station in Red Lion, Pennsylvania, which devoted most of its programming to fundamentalist religion. One program featured the Reverend Billy James Hargis. Like McIntire, Hargis often used his time to castigate those he considered to be liberals. Here is what he broadcast about a New York newspaperman and author named Fred Cook.

Now who is Cook? Cook was fired from the New York World-Telegram after he made a false charge publicly on television against an unnamed official of the New York City government. New York publishers and Newsweek magazine for December 7, 1959 showed that Fred Cook and his pal Eugene Gleason had made up the whole story, and this confession was made to District Attorney Frank Hogan.[12]

Cook requested time from the station for a reply to the attack. Norris sent him his commercial rate card. Hargis had paid for his time; Cook must do likewise, regardless of what the FCC might have said in the Cullman case. Cook complained to the commission. It found Norris to be in violation of the fairness doctrine and its personal attack policy. Norris appealed to the courts. In a notable decision released in 1969 the U.S. Supreme Court unanimously upheld the fairness doctrine and the personal attack rule confounding those broadcasters and their lawyers who for years had asserted that both were unconstitutional.

A brief explanation of the personal attack rule is due here. It originally evolved as a commission policy that was described as a "particularization" of the fairness doctrine. Later it became a formal commission rule. It may be summarized as follows.

If, during the discussion of a controversial public issue, a station broadcasts an attack upon the "honesty, character, integrity or like personal qualities of an identified person or group," it must send a copy of the attack to that person or group, together with an offer of its facilities for a reply to the attack.[13]

Not every criticism, no matter how harsh, is a personal attack under the rule. It must impugn the "honesty, character [or] integrity" of its target. The commission has held that calling someone a liar, coward, arsonist, thief, cheat, traitor, or terrorist is an attack, but charging that he is a law violator, "inefficient," "obnoxious," "a confirmed nuisance," a "political opportunist," or even an incompetent physician is not.

There are a number of exceptions to the rule. It does not apply, for example, to attacks broadcast by political candidates or to attacks broadcast during news programs or to "commentary or analysis contained within such programs."

The Communications Act prohibits broadcasters from censoring anything that a candidate may say, no matter how false or libelous,[14] so it is only fair that broadcasters not be held liable for their fulminations.

There is sound reason, also, for exempting newscasts. If the rule applied to them, and if a news item came in on the wire shortly before scheduled airtime to the effect that Senator Smidge had accused another official (or anyone else) of embezzlement, the news director might feel that the item must be rejected or at least postponed until he or she could make sure that the object of the attack could be located so as to send him or her a copy of the story and an invitation to respond to it. A substantial part of news programming consists of material that borders on personal attacks, and because of the number of them and ever-present deadlines, a great burden would be thrown on newspeople if they had to weigh every item in light of the personal attack rule.

There is no such justification for exempting "commentary or analysis contained within" news programs. Commentary almost always is written long before broadcast time, so the commentator has full opportunity to consider whether anything he or she wants to say might be a personal attack under the rule and, if so, what obligations would be incurred. The commission added the commentary exemption to its list for reasons of expedience rather than logic, during the backstage maneuvering that preceded the Red Lion decision. Had logic prevailed, the exemption should have included commentary broadcast outside of hard news programs as well as within.

The artful dodges that the opposing sides used in Red Lion may be of interest. After the FCC ruled against him Norris took his case to the Circuit Court of Appeals for the District of Columbia Circuit, where he lost. The National Association of Broadcasters, which had contributed ten thousand dollars to his appellate expenses, was reluctant to have the case go to the Supreme Court and to have the constitutionality of the fairness doctrine decided on the basis of such a weak set of facts. It tried to dissuade Norris from a further appeal, but he refused to quit.

However, soon after the D.C. circuit court had upheld its Red Lion ruling, the FCC unwittingly provided other opponents of the fairness doctrine with a way to get in on the action. The FCC voted to convert its personal attack *policy* into a specific *rule,* which would enable it to punish violation with either license revocation or the lesser sanction of a monetary forfeiture.[15]

Standing on the sidelines and waiting to enter the game was Ted Pierson, a well-known Washington communications attorney and counsel for the Radio-Television News Directors' Association. Pierson had long proclaimed the fairness doctrine to be unconstitutional, and he saw in the commission's adoption of the personal attack rule an opportunity to challenge it on behalf of the news directors rather than for some huge corporate entity like a network. However, CBS and NBC wanted part of the action, too. Each announced that it also would challenge the rule.

Pierson chose to file his plea in the Seventh Circuit Court of Appeals in Chicago because that court was generally regarded as unsympathetic to federal regulation. This was an example of the custom among lawyers of shopping around for a court that is likely to favor their viewpoint. CBS and NBC elected to take their cases to the Second Circuit Court in New York.

Now ensued an unseemly race to become the first to file and thus ensure that the case would be heard by the preferred court. Pierson filed his challenge in the Seventh Circuit Court shortly before noon (central time) on July 27, 1967. CBS didn't get its papers to the New York court until 4:50 P.M. (eastern time) on the same day. (NBC filed four days later.) Under federal rules all three similar cases were consolidated for consideration by the court where the filing first took place—Chicago.

Somewhat uneasy over these developments, the FCC decided to amend its newly adopted personal attack rule to exempt news broadcasts. This wasn't enough for the Department of Justice, which was at that time headed by Ramsey Clark. The Justice Department has the duty to defend other federal agencies when their decisions are appealed, but it began dragging its feet about joining the FCC in this case, just as it did in the George Carlin indecent language case described in Chapter 3. The department's attorneys apparently were intimidated by the CBS claims that the doctrine had a "chilling effect" on journalism—especially the CBS protests against applying the personal attack rule to Eric Sevareid's analysis on the CBS nightly news. The Justice Department said it would not join the FCC in the Supreme Court appeal unless the rule were further amended.

The commission obediently added the news analysis exemption.[16] Commissioner Lee Loevinger declared that this made no sense. He dubbed it "the Eric Sevareid amendment." (Incidentally, in its subsequent Red Lion decision the Supreme Court gave no indication that the rule amendments played any part in the decision.)

The Cigarette Case and Where It Led

One of the FCC's boldest ventures in administering the fairness doctrine was its ill-fated effort to apply it to cigarette advertising. Twenty years after the Reverend Sam Morris lost his complaint against wine and beer ads, a young Columbia University Law School graduate named John Banzhaf III filed one against CBS because its New York TV station had rejected his request that it give free time for viewpoints in contrast to those expressed in its cigarette advertising.

Banzhaf took his case to the FCC, which astounded the broadcasting industry by holding for the first time that the fairness doctrine could apply to commercial product advertising.[17] The commission found that a station presenting cigarette advertising "has the duty of informing its audience of the other side of the issue . . . that, however enjoyable, such smoking may be a hazard to the smoker's health." The commission leaned heavily on the fact that the 1964 report of the U.S. surgeon general's Advisory Committee on Smoking and Health had found cigarette smoking to be a hazard to human health and that Congress, in the Federal Cigarette Labeling and Advertising Act, had required manufacturers to carry this message on each pack. In an effort to limit the scope of its revolutionary ruling the commission dwelt heavily on the uniqueness of the case. It said it could conceive of no other product that would bring about a like ruling.

In applying the doctrine to cigarette advertising the commission ignored the fact that the commercials made no claim that smoking was healthful or that the surgeon general's report was wrong. It said that the ads portrayed smoking as a pleasurable, socially acceptable experience and therefore, *by implication,* presented a partisan viewpoint on a controversial issue of public importance.

The decision prompted another race to the courts. The National Association of Broadcasters and the cigarette manufacturers decided to file their appeals in the Fourth Circuit Court. Being located in Richmond, Virginia, it was presumed to be sympathetic to the views of the tobacco-growers and cigarette manufacturers that surrounded it.

Banzhaf was quicker on the draw. He had won his case with the commission but he found a reason to file his own appeal on the grounds that the commission should have granted "equal time" for antismoking messages (which it had never done in a fairness case). His reason for appealing was that he wanted all of the appeals to be heard by the D.C. Circuit Court, which he rightly suspected would be more inclined to affirm the commission ruling than the Richmond court. He managed to get his plea filed first and thus won the race. The consolidated appeal was thereafter labeled *Banzhaf et al.* v. *FCC,* although the two nominal opponents were on the same side.

The D.C. court affirmed the commission's ruling, although it, too, went to considerable lengths to limit its scope. Chief Judge David Bazelon stated that the holding was limited to one product, cigarettes. He wrote, "We emphasize that our cautious approval of this particular decision does not license the Commission to scan the airwaves for offensive material with no more discriminating a lens than the 'public interest' or even the 'public health.' "[18]

The commission soon learned that this disclaimer meant little. As might have been expected, the cigarette decision prompted other efforts to obtain free counter-commercials to radio-television advertising. Fairness doctrine complaints were filed against ads for snowmobiles (which allegedly raised environmental issues), trash compactors (said to discourage recycling of containers), and even Crest toothpaste.

The commission turned down all attempts to expand the cigarette decision. In rejecting a complaint against an ad for Chevron gasoline, it said

Making a claim for a product is not the same thing as arguing a position on a controversial issue of public importance. . . . It would ill suit the purposes of the fairness doctrine, designed to illumine significant controversial issues, to apply it to claims of a product's efficacy or social utility. The merits of any one gasoline, weight reducer, breakfast cereal or headache remedy — to name but a few examples that come to mind — do not rise to the level of a significant public issue.[19]

With this reductio ad absurdum the FCC thought it had disposed of the issue, but it underestimated the capriciousness of the D.C. Circuit Court of Appeals.

A subsequent complaint asked application of the fairness doctrine to advertisements for large cars on the grounds that their exhaust caused more atmospheric pollution than small cars. (This prompted some wags at the commission to ask whether Friends of the Earth, the environmentalist group that filed the complaint, wanted each ad for a Cadillac offset by one for a Volkswagen.)

Consistent with its decision in the Chevron case, the commission denied this complaint,[20] referring to its "previous judgment that cigarettes are a unique product." But to its dismay, the D.C. Circuit Court did an about-face and said it could "find no plausible difference" between the auto commercials and cigarette advertising since, it said, both types urged use of products that had built-in health hazards.[21]

The court did offer the FCC a way of escape from its dilemma. It noted that the commission had begun an inquiry into the application of the fairness doctrine. However, it said that "pending . . . reformulation of [the FCC's] position" the court was finding the Friends of the Earth complaint indistinguishable from that of Banzhaf.[22]

This hint that the court might support the commission in a new approach toward relieving the headache that the Banzhaf case had induced was not lost on the commission. Chairman Dean Burch had appointed a committee to reexamine the whole fairness doctrine and restate the commission's policies in administering it. This committee, headed by General Counsel Richard Wiley, wrote the *Fairness Report,* which the commission adopted in 1974.[23]

In this document the commission confessed that it had erred in making its cigarette ruling, especially in view of the fact that the D.C. Circuit Court had refused to limit the precedent to that product. Said the commission,

It seems to us to make little practical sense to view advertisements such as these as presenting a meaningful discussion of a controversial issue of public importance. . . . Accordingly, in the future we will apply the fairness doctrine only to those "commercials" which are devoted in an obvious and meaningful way to the discussion of public issues.[24]

Thus ended the flap over product advertising and a policy that had resulted in a wholesale exodus from the air of cigarette advertisers. They understandably could not see their way to subsidizing free radio-TV advertisements against their products, when they could buy space in the print media without triggering rejoinders.

At any rate, the issue had become moot when Congress adopted a law banning cigarette advertising from the air as of January 2, 1971.

The Commissioners Roll Some Logs

The commission now moved from disputes about application of the fairness doctrine to product advertising to its application to what had become the most important issue of the time: American participation in the Vietnam War. In August 1970 the commission released a decision disposing of complaints based on network TV broadcasts about the war. One complaint was filed against the networks for their alleged failure to give adequate opportunity for replies to five prime-time TV addresses made by President Richard Nixon between November 3, 1969, and June 3, 1970, in which he defended the administration's position on the war in Indochina.

The commission ruled that, although normally a licensee had almost unlimited latitude in choosing how to meet its obligations under the fairness doctrine, a more exacting standard was appropriate when someone with the prestige of a president made five uninterrupted prime-time television appearances advocating one side of the same issue. Therefore, said the FCC, each network should provide at least one prime-time period for uninterrupted expression of contrasting views on the issue.[25] Although this ruling was unusual, it was not unreasonable in light of the circumstances. What was unusual was the way in which the commission arrived at it: namely, by logrolling among some Republican and Democratic commissioners[26] in an agreement to approve both it and a Republican National Committee (RNC) complaint against a broadcast on CBS by Lawrence O'Brien, chairman of the Democratic National Committee (DNC).[27]

In view of President Nixon's frequent use of prime-time TV to advocate his causes,[28] CBS had offered twenty-five minutes of time to O'Brien for a series of "Loyal Opposition" broadcasts in which the Democrats were to give their views on current issues. O'Brien made his first — and only — broadcast on July 7, 1970, in which he gave the DNC position on the Vietnam War, as well as on the economy, civil rights, the crime problem, air and water pollution, and federal expenditures for defense.

One day later the chairman of the Republican National Committee requested time from CBS to reply to O'Brien. It argued that the broadcast had been a political attack on the president and his party instead of an "issue-oriented response."

On August 18 the commission ruled in the RNC's favor. It said CBS had failed to exercise "journalistic supervision to assure fulfillment of its purpose" of allowing the opposition party an opportunity to reply to the president on major issues discussed in prior presidential appearances. It said Nixon's speeches had "largely concentrated" on the Indochina war issue, and CBS should have compelled O'Brien to concentrate on this issue.[29] In a petition for reconsideration, the DNC stated that neither it nor CBS ever had intended that O'Brien's broadcasts should be limited to the war issue, and that O'Brien's references to other issues were in response to presidential broadcasts on these issues.

In conformity with its prior agreement, the commission majority denied a plea for reconsideration and the DNC and CBS took their case to the D.C. Circuit Court.

On November 15, 1971, the court released a decision reversing the commission with some of the harshest language it ever had used. The opinion, written by Judge J. Skelly Wright, said, among other uncomplimentary things,

We conclude, therefore, that the [FCC] ruling . . . marked as it is by a succession of factual distortions and shifting justifications, must be reversed.[30]

Judge Edward Tamm agreed saying, "They [the commissioners] have created a debacle in seeking a sound basis for this decision."[31]

Wright could find no reason under the fairness doctrine why CBS should have limited O'Brien to the war issue or why the FCC should have claimed that his broadcast should be aimed only at the five speeches in which President Nixon had discussed the war. The president had discussed many other issues in other television appearances. So had other members of his administration.

Some of the court's strongest language was directed at the gyrations the commission had gone through in trying to justify the ruling. Tamm charged the commission with changing its legal position three times in trying to justify the original ruling—first, in denying the plea for reconsideration; second, in its brief to the court; and third, in oral argument before the court.

The court made it clear that it was not placing the blame for the commission's faults on Daniel R. Ohlbaum, FCC deputy general counsel, who argued the case before the court for the commission.[32] The truth is that both Ohlbaum and General Counsel Henry Geller had been at their wits' end in trying to rationalize an irrational ruling. Geller had written the commission's original ruling and the denial of the plea for reconsideration. Ohlbaum had been saddled with the task of making the oral argument and had decided that none of the previous FCC documents was defensible, so he had thought up an entirely new line of defense in a vain effort to save the case.

The Controversy Continues

It is somewhat ironic that a doctrine designed to deal with controversial public issues became itself one of the most controversial of issues within the broadcast industry.

NBC, CBS, the National Association of Broadcasters, and the hierarchies of some journalistic organizations claimed the fairness doctrine tended to limit freedom of press and speech. When pressed for examples, they usually took refuge in vague assertions that it had "a chilling effect" on journalism—an effect that might not be apparent to the outsider but that nevertheless afflicted the journalists.

One might conclude, then, that the individual radio and television news directors would believe the doctrine to be a serious encumbrance to their efforts to report the news. However, this has not been true of those on the firing line—the station news directors who operate under the doctrine in making their daily decisions.

The Radio-Television News Directors Association made two surveys of its membership, as reported in its publication, the *RTNDA Communicator.* One survey was made in 1972, the other in 1982. The surveys covered television and radio stations of all sizes. They asked news directors what they believed their principal problems to be.[33]

In the 1972 survey the number one problem turned out to be budgetary—getting enough money from management to operate their departments properly. Problem number two was obtaining adequate equipment such as mobile units, film and videotape cameras, and shortwave links from field positions to their newsrooms. Number three was "maintaining a qualified staff."

The least important problems (numbers six and seven) were the fairness doctrine and the equal time law for political candidates. Although 47 percent of news directors thought budgets were a major problem, 36 percent believed equipment to be a major one, and 31 percent put staffing in this category, only 5 percent ranked the fairness doctrine and the equal time law as major problems. Among radio station news directors, only 1 percent considered either fairness or equal time to be a major problem.

The results of the 1982 RTNDA survey were almost identical. Forty-eight percent of TV news directors ranked budgetary matters as a major problem; 41 percent named equipment; and

32 percent, staffing. Only 2 percent now considered either fairness or equal time to be such a problem. Among radio news directors, the figure was 1 percent.

Seventy-five percent of TV news directors said fairness was no problem at all, and 23 percent thought it was only a minor problem. Among radio station news editors, 88 percent thought fairness to be no problem at all, and 11 percent ranked it as a minor one.

To me, these figures belie the claims of those who have attacked the doctrine as an infringement of free speech or press or claim it has a chilling effect.

There are, of course, some criticisms of the doctrine that may rightfully be made. One is that its very name has misled members of the public into thinking that their fairness complaints will have some result, whereas, for the reasons set forth at the beginning of this chapter, very few have. In practice, the doctrine has been applied only to the most egregious violations and, even then, only when the complainants met the FCC's rigid threshold requirements for filing complaints.

Another valid criticism is that the doctrine is hard to administer and could be misused by a biased commission. It is indeed sometimes difficult to determine (1) whether a controversial issue of public importance has been presented in a program, (2) whether only one side was presented, and (3) whether the licensee's judgment was reasonable. However, the fact that a biased commission might misuse this regulation is no more true of this part of broadcast law than of any other part. When the FCC did let political considerations influence its action in the RNC-DNC-CBS case cited earlier, the court of appeals quickly set it back on its heels.

I believe that, on the whole, the fairness doctrine had a salutary effect on broadcasting. Most broadcasters doubtless would try to present contrasting views on controversial issues even if there were no regulations in this area, but some would not.

In justice to the commission, it should be added that most of the cases cited in this chapter were not typical of its conduct in administering the doctrine between 1962 and 1980. On the whole, it did an honest, conscientious, intelligent job of attempting to administer a most difficult form of regulation.

The FCC Decides to Scuttle the Doctrine

Shortly after Ronald Reagan appointed Mark Fowler chairman of the commission it began trying to abandon most regulation of broadcasting including the fairness doctrine. (See Chapter 8.) In September 1981 the FCC recommended to Congress that the doctrine be repealed.[34] In May 1984 it issued a notice of inquiry into general fairness doctrine obligations of broadcast licensees. Its announced purpose was to reexamine the rationale for the doctrine and inquire into its effects.[35] This was only ten years after the FCC, also under a Republican chairman, had found in its 1974 *Fairness Report* that the legality of the doctrine had been established by the Supreme Court in Red Lion and had "re-affirmed the basic validity and soundness of these principles and policies."

To no one's surprise, the new inquiry resulted in a report that the doctrine no longer served the public interest because "the development of the information services marketplace makes unnecessary any governmentally imposed obligation to provide balanced coverage of controversial issues of public importance."[36] The report also found that the doctrine had a "chilling effect on broadcasters' speech." However, the commission decided not to eliminate the doctrine "at this time."[37] One question that seemed to deter the FCC from outright abrogation of the doctrine was whether the Supreme Court in Red Lion had found that Congress had made it a part of the Communications Act when it amended Section 315(a) to exempt from the equal time requirement appearances by political candidates on news programs. In so doing, Congress added this language: "Nothing in the foregoing sentence shall be construed as relieving broadcasters . . . from the obligation imposed upon them under this Act to operate in the public interest and to afford reasonable opportunity for the discussion of conflicting views on issues of public importance."

With respect to this passage, the Red Lion court said, "Here the Congress has not just kept its silence by refusing to overturn the administrative construction, but has ratified it with positive legislation."[38]

At another point in its decision, the Court said the amendment

makes it very plain that Congress, in 1959, announced that the phrase "public interest," which had been in the Act since 1927, imposed a duty on broadcasters to discuss both sides of controversial public issues. In other words, the amendment vindicated the FCC's general view that the fairness doctrine inhered in the public interest standard.

Moreover, in another case four years later, the Court stated, "in 1959, Congress amended Section 315 of the Act to give statutory approval of the Fairness Doctrine.[39]

For years Red Lion was considered as having established that the 1959 amendment made the fairness doctrine a part of the *law,* not merely a valid FCC *policy;* but some dissenters claimed that the Court merely meant that Congress did not want to rescind the FCC's existing fairness *policy.* As might be expected, the commission under Fowler chose to believe that "the United States Supreme Court so far has not given a definite answer on whether or not the fairness doctrine has been explicitly codified into the Communications Act."

A year later, the commission's efforts to get rid of the doctrine were given a considerable boost in a decision of the D.C. Circuit Court of Appeals written by Judge Robert Bork[40] in *Telecommunications and Research Action Center* v. *FCC,* which stated,

We do not believe that language adopted in 1959 made the fairness doctrine a binding statutory obligation; rather, it ratified the Commission's longstanding position that the public interest standard authorizes the fairness doctrine. . . . Congress described the obligation . . . as one "imposed . . . *under the Act,*" 47 U.S.C. 315(a) [emphasis added] not by the Act.[41]

Thus, Judge Bork based his decision on the fact that Congress had used the word "under" rather than "by." And if, as he held, the 1959 amendment merely *authorized* the commission to promulgate the fairness doctrine, the commission was presumably free to change its mind and decide that the public interest standard no longer required fairness in broadcasting.

The appellants petitioned for a rehearing of the case by the entire eleven-judge court of appeals, but a rehearing en banc is granted only if a majority of the entire eleven-judge court votes for it. In this case, two of the judges did not participate in the vote, and although five of the remaining nine voted "aye," rehearing was denied.

The en banc petition gave one of the judges, Abner Mikva, an opportunity to write a strong dissent to Bork's original opinion.[42] Mikva said the ruling was "flatly wrong" and that Congress, in amending the act in 1959, "explicitly approved of, ratified and codified the fairness doctrine."

Mikva cited the legislative history of the 1959 amendment in support of his position. One passage he cited was from the Senate Communications Subcommittee report on the bill. It stated that the proposed amendment would not affect commission "policy or existing law, which holds that a licensee's *statutory obligation* to serve the public interest" includes the duty to present "a fair cross section of opinion." Another passage was from a statement by Senator John Pastore, chairman of the subcommittee. Pastore declared "I understand the amendment to be a statement or codification of the standards of fairness." A third example was an excerpt from the Senate-House conference report on the bill that said it was "a restatement of the basic policy of the 'standard of fairness' which is imposed on broadcasters under [the Act]." Finally, the chairman of the House committee that sponsored the bill had said it "reaffirmed the 'standard of fairness' established under the [Act]."

Mikva also quoted the Supreme Court in Red Lion to the effect that the 1959 amendment had "ratified" the FCC's construction of the public interest standard "with positive legislation," and the Court's statement in another case that Congress had imposed on all broadcast licensees "an affirmative and independent statutory obligation to provide full and fair coverage of public issues."[43]

Bork, who had ignored the legislative history of the 1959 amendment in his opinion in the TRAC case, now issued a statement in defense of his ruling.[44] He said, "Many of the remarks culled from the legislative history by the dissent are either ambiguous on the question before us or are read most easily as mere approvals of the Commission's exercise of its delegated authority." He said the Supreme Court had considered the legislative history in Red Lion and since, in Bork's opinion, that court had merely affirmed the FCC's authority to promulgate the doctrine as its own policy rather than under a congressional mandate, that was that! He repeated his original claim that since the amendment stated that the fairness doctrine was imposed "under" the act rather than "by" the act, it did not make the doctrine a statutory obligation.

Meanwhile, realizing what the commission was up to, the Senate Committee on Commerce, Science and Transportation reported favorably a bill to make the fairness doctrine an unquestionable requirement of the act.[45] The Senate passed the bill on April 21, 1987, and the House on June 3, but President Reagan vetoed it on June 19.[46] The Senate voted to return the bill to committee rather than try to override the veto.[47]

Seeing its chance, at long last, to apply the coup de grace, the commission on August 4, 1987, adopted a memorandum opinion and order declaring the fairness doctrine unconstitutional![48]

The FCC was given the opportunity to concoct this decision (in an area clearly the prerogative of the appellate courts) by the D.C. Circuit Court of Appeals, which already had obligingly ruled that the fairness doctrine was not a part of the Communications Act. Not long after Judge Bork wrote that decision, the court remanded another case to the commission with instructions that it consider the station's claim that the fairness doctrine was unconstitutional.[49] (Incidentally, the remanded case[50] was the *only* fairness ruling the commission had made against a station since Ronald Reagan had become president.)

In its new ruling on the remanded case, the commission said that times had changed in the eighteen years since the Supreme Court had voted unanimously that the doctrine was constitutional. The doctrine had a chilling effect on broadcast licensees (a contention that the Supreme Court had considered and rejected). More importantly, said the commission, there were now more stations than when Red Lion was decided—54 percent more TV stations and 57 percent more radio stations—so there no longer was need to regulate broadcasts because of the scarcity of electronic sources of information, especially in view of the growth of cable and satellite television.

However, the commission could not ignore the fact that the principal justification cited by the Supreme Court for upholding the doctrine was the scarcity of frequencies rather than of individual stations. As Justice Byron White had written for the Court, there are "substantially more individuals who want to broadcast than there are frequencies to allocate."[51] Therefore,

As far as the First Amendment is concerned those who are licensed stand no better than those to whom licenses are refused. A license permits broadcasting, but the licensee has no constitutional right to be the one who holds the license or to monopolize a radio frequency to the exclusion of his fellow citizens. There is nothing in the First Amendment which prevents the Government from requiring a licensee to share his frequency with others and to conduct himself as a proxy or fiduciary with obligations to present those views and voices which are representative of his community and which would otherwise, by necessity, be barred from the airwaves.[52]

In an attempt to counter this rationale, the FCC again cited language of Judge Bork in the TRAC case. In dealing with the question of scarcity of spectrum, he had, in effect, accused the Supreme Court of "analytical confusion." Bork noted that "the Court found justification for limiting first amendment protection of broadcasting in the 'scarcity doctrine' " (p. 507). Farther along in his opinion, he stated

It is certainly true that broadcast frequencies are scarce but it is unclear why that fact justifies content regulation of broadcasting that would be intolerable if applied to the editorial process of the print media. All economic goods are scarce. . . . Since scarcity is a universal fact, it can hardly explain regulation in one context and not another. The attempt to use a universal fact as a distinguishing principle necessarily leads to analytical confusion (p. 508, footnotes omitted).

The FCC now added its own ten-cents' worth and said, "we believe it would be desirable for the Supreme Court to reconsider its use of a constitutional standard based upon spectrum scarcity."

Thus did the commission dispose of the fairness doctrine —
at least, for the present. Appeals of the decision were filed by
the Syracuse Peace Council, the Office of Communication of
the United Church of Christ, the Communication Commission
of the National Council of Churches, and by Henry Geller and
Donna Lampert of the Washington Center for Public Policy
Research.

The brief filed by Geller and Lampert for themselves and
the Syracuse Peace Council asserted that the FCC decision un-
dermines the entire public trustee concept of broadcasting man-
dated by Congress and upheld by the Supreme Court. Only the
Supreme Court itself, it said, can declare the public trustee approach unconstitutional, not the FCC, which, it asserted, had
"simply shaped its decision to its own ideological bent" while
"glibly making up reasons for dumping the fairness doctrine."

Under the FCC decision, the brief pointed out, any station
owner might hereafter broadcast only those viewpoints on
public issues with which the owner agreed or for which he or she
was paid. Moreover, as Judge Bork pointed out in his TRAC
opinion, the Supreme Court in Red Lion "expressly noted that
the equal-time provision of Section 315 [of the Act] was 'indistinguishable' . . . 'in terms of constitutional principle' from the
implementing regulations of the fairness doctrine before the
court. 395 U.S. at 391"[53] Bork again had recognized this in a
1987 circuit court decision in which he refused to declare the
equal time law invalid on constitutional grounds because, he
said, "the *Red Lion* decision on the constitutionality of fairness
also controls the constitutionality of equal time."[54]

As to the commission's claim that the fairness doctrine had
such a chilling effect on broadcasters as to reduce their coverage
of constitutional issues, the Geller-Lampert brief noted that the
Supreme Court found the doctrine had no such overall effect
and that after a two-year study, the FCC in its 1974 *Fairness
Report* found "no credible evidence" to support such a claim. As
recently as 1987, the concerned committees of both the House
and Senate had arrived at the same conclusion.[55]

The commission's decision to kill the fairness doctrine was,
somewhat surprisingly, upheld in February 1989 by the Circuit
Court of Appeals for the District of Columbia Circuit.[56] In Sep-

tember 1989 the appellants filed a petition for certiorari with the U.S. Supreme Court.

Whether or not the Supreme Court acts to resurrect the doctrine, it appears that Congress will enact a law to do so, since such a new bill has been reported favorably by committees in both houses. Given the positive and long-standing support that Congress has given the doctrine, the odds would seem to favor reinstatement of it.

5

The Radio Medicine Men

Bad as present-day broadcast programming may be, it has at least been purged by the government of many of the frauds that beset early radio.

One source of revenue in the first decade of broadcasting was the peripatetic fortune-teller who moved from station to station, flimflamming the public in each market. The fortune-tellers would broadcast an answer to any question mailed to them for two dollars (originally, one dollar). One advertisement said, "Send a question you want answered and Moo Moo with the Second Sight will answer it. Send your name, birth date, and a sample of your handwriting."

Typical answers included: "Don't marry that man. It will mean nothing but trouble. I believe he has a terrible disease." "Buy the stock you mention. You will make about $2,000 on the deal within 65 days." "It appears to me that the man you say you love has spent time in a penitentiary."[1]

Many other kinds of fraudulent advertising flourished, from penny-a-day burial insurance to "guaranteed" cures for all bodily ailments.

For purposes of illustration, the author has chosen the two most notorious medical quacks of the period.

Doc Brinkley and His Goat-Gland Operation

Of all of the frauds who have used the airwaves to bilk the public, none was more colorful or successful than John Richard "Doc" Brinkley, the celebrated goat-gland surgeon of Milford, Kansas, and Del Rio, Texas.[2]

Brinkley was the first medical charlatan to sense the full potentialities of radio. During a broadcasting career of almost eighteen years that began in 1923 he grossed up to four million dollars annually. When he filed a libel suit in 1939 against an official of the American Medical Association (AMA), he charged that unfavorable articles about him in an AMA magazine had reduced his net personal income from more than a million dollars to a mere $810,000 a year.

Brinkley wore diamonds worth $100,000 and owned a dozen Cadillacs, a private plane, and three yachts ranging up to 150 feet in size. His assets also included a Texas ranch, oil wells, and of course, a powerful radio station that made everything else possible.

The Doc is best known for having popularized his goat-gland operation. For sums ranging from $750 to $1,500, he transplanted parts of the glands of Toggenburg goats to the organs of older men who felt in need of rejuvenation. Doc's credentials to practice medicine consisted of a diploma obtained in 1915 from "The Eclectic Medical University of Kansas City."

The AMA was not impressed by Brinkley's credentials and it denounced his goat-gland operation as worthless, but the power of radio advertising and a longing for the vanished pleasures of youth caused thousands of suckers to flock to the village of Milford, Kansas, and later to Del Rio, Texas, some of them mortgaging their homes to help fill Doc's coffers. The Brinkley policy was cash on the barrelhead.

Brinkley obtained the license for Station KFKB in 1923. He got the idea of using radio to advertise his operation from Harry Chandler, owner of the *Los Angeles Times,* on whom Doc had performed his goat-gland operation. KFKB meant "Kansas Folks Know Best," Brinkley would explain. At other times he said the call letters stood for "Kansas First, Kansas Best."

The station drew a large audience and attracted thousands to Milford for the operation. Brinkley not only advertised his surgical services on the air; he preached "sermons" that were cribbed from Giovanni Papini's *Life of Christ*. Also, he prescribed cures for every imaginable ailment of his radio audience. The station boasted other attractions. For one dollar, someone called "Tea-Leaf Kitty from Jersey City" would answer any three questions sent to her. The daughter of the Milford barber was the Tell-Me-a-Story Lady of KFKB, relating the adventures of Little Cuffy Bear. The sheriff's daughter was the Doc's secretary. The local newspaper editor did Doc's job printing. Yes, Brinkley gave new life in more ways than one to sleepy little Milford.

Doc finally lost his radio license, not because of the goat-gland operation but because of a program in which he diagnosed the illnesses of thousands of persons he had never seen and prescribed his own medical remedies for their relief. For this phase of his service to mankind, Doc set up the Brinkley Pharmaceutical Association (wholly owned by Brinkley), which any pharmacist in the nation could join if he or she agreed to make a kickback to Brinkley on the sale of each Brinkley prescription. Brinkley broadcast "The Medical Question Box" three times a day, diagnosing ailments and prescribing remedies on the basis of symptoms described in letters from far and near. Brinkley always prescribed one or more of his own prescriptions, which were designated by number.

Two examples of Doc's instant diagnoses come from the opinion of the U.S. Circuit Court of Appeals, which affirmed the Federal Radio Commission's eventual revocation of the KFKB license.[3]

Here's one from Tillie. She says she had an operation, had some trouble ten years ago. I think the operation was unnecessary, and it isn't very good sense to have an ovary removed with the expectation of motherhood resulting therefrom. My advice to you is to use Women's Tonic No. 50, 67 and 61.

Sunflower State—from Dresden, Kansas. Probably he has gallstones. No, I don't mean that. I mean kidney stones. My advice to you is to put him on Prescription No. 80 and 50 for men, also, 64.

The druggists who joined the Brinkley Pharmaceutical Association were the only ones who knew what the Doc's numbered prescriptions were, so they enjoyed a monopoly of the radio trade, selling compounds for sums ranging from $3.50 to $10.00 but having to kick back a dollar to the Doc on each one. Some of the druggists may not have slept too well at night, but they often took in more from the numbered concoctions than from filling the prescriptions of the local doctors in their communities.

At last, not only the American Medical Association but the Kansas Medical Association and the powerful *Kansas City Star* took after Brinkley and got both his Kansas medical license and his KFKB radio license revoked. The Federal Radio Commission refused to renew the station license because it concluded that "the operation of KFKB is conducted only in the interest of Dr. Brinkley" rather than in the public interest, as the law was supposed to require. The FRC said that prescribing medicine for a patient one has never seen and basing the diagnosis on symptoms recited in a letter "is inimical to the public health and safety."

Doc didn't give up without a fight. He charged that the authorities were out to get him. To the radio commission, he pleaded the First Amendment's guarantee of free speech. He sued Dr. Morris Fishbein of the AMA for $600,000 and later for $250,000, but lost both times. He went on the air and announced that he would take five thousand satisfied ex-patients to Washington at his expense to tell the radio commission they had been cured of all ills. Later he reduced the scope of the offer and said he would pay expenses for one thousand persons. Still later he said there would be a Pullman train ready for all who wanted to accompany him to Washington—at their own expense. One carload of Brinkley fans did go. The radio commission, fearing an influx, moved the hearing to an auditorium in the Interior Department building.

The witnesses for Brinkley included a Kansas lady who vowed that prescription no. 150 was "not only good. It's wonderful." She said all ten members of her family had been using it (presumably, all suffering from the same malady). Brinkley also produced 1,400 affidavits on his behalf, but on June 30, 1930, the FRC denied renewal of his license,[4] and after an unsuccessful appeal to the courts, Brinkley made his final broadcast on KFKB in February 1931. He described the demise of the station as a blow to free speech.

Meanwhile, Brinkley had run for governor of Kansas in November 1930 in an effort at vindication. His slogan was "Let's pasture the goats on the State House lawn." He promised free school books and auto licenses and a lake in every county of that somewhat arid state. He explained that the water, which would be evaporated from the lakes and precipitated as rainfall, would make Kansas a modern Canaan. As an independent, Brinkley filed too late to get on the ballot and had to run as a write-in candidate. Under the stringent laws of the state, persons voting for a write-in candidate were required to spell his name exactly right and to comply with other highly technical requirements. At each campaign stop around the state that fall, Brinkley would begin the rally by leading a yell which consisted of spelling out "B-R-I-N-K-L-E-Y," in an effort to teach his followers how to write his name on the ballot. Despite the write-in handicap, Brinkley ran second in a three-man field, beating the Republican candidate. He even got twenty thousand votes in neighboring Oklahoma against "Alfalfa Bill" Murray.

Brinkley ran for governor again in 1932, using a radio station owned by a Wichita insurance company as his mouthpiece. Although he lost to Republican Alf Landon, he carried more counties than either Landon or the incumbent Democrat, Harry M. Woodring. His opponents were hardly nonentities, either. Landon became GOP presidential candidate in 1936, and Woodring was Franklin D. Roosevelt's secretary of war.

After he lost his Kansas medical license and KFKB, Brinkley moved his base of operations to Del Rio, Texas, just across the Rio Grande from Villa Acuna, Mexico, where he took over Station XERA. It became the most powerful station in the world with 500,000 watts.[5] It sprayed its signal far and wide over the North American continent, bearing the good tidings that Brinkley had transferred the scene of his boundless benefits to the little town of Del Rio. Reporter Bob Casey wrote in the *Chicago Daily News* that its signal was so strong that it could "light the street lights in Calgary."[6] Brinkley had another priceless advantage with his new transmitter. He could switch wavelengths at will and blanket the signals of various U.S. stations, which had to stick to their assigned frequencies and limit their power to a range of 100 to 50,000 watts.

For the time being, the Mexican government did not interfere, in part because, up to this time, Mexico had never been able to get the United States to negotiate seriously for an international treaty to allocate radio frequencies between the two countries. Thus, Mexico used XERA as a club to force the United States to come to the bargaining table.

In response, Washington finally suggested a North American Radio Conference, which was held in Mexico City in 1933, but former vice-president Charles Curtis (a fellow Kansan) rushed there to use his influence on the Doc's behalf, and nothing was accomplished. In 1934, Brinkley did have to switch to another Mexican station, but by 1935, after another change in governments, he was back at XERA.

It might be well for those who denounce all government radio regulation to consider the unregulated programming of XERA in the 1930s. First, Brinkley had taken to advertising a prostate gland operation, which replaced the goat-gland surgery as his principal source of revenue. He charged a flat $750 for the surgery. He solicited testimonials from former patients by offering a new car to the best letter beginning, "I consider Dr. Brinkley the world's foremost prostate specialist because . . . " He also continued to broadcast prescriptions for patients he had never seen.

Among his advertisements were rupture cures, anointed cloths, bargains in gravestones, electric bow ties, penny-a-day burial insurance, and gold mine stocks.

Brinkley's cast included a crystal-gazer named Koran, Rose Dawn, an astrologer, and the Reverend Sam Morris (see Chapter 4), who advocated the return of Prohibition and sought contributions with which to build a radio station to advance that cause.

Brinkley ran a hospital in Del Rio, and between 1933 and 1938 it treated 16,000 patients and grossed twelve million dollars. This money was in addition to the income Brinkley earned from his various other enterprises.

From 1937 on, Brinkley's broadcasts became more and more isolationist in tone. "Send a few dollars to the antiwar fund," he would plead. He found himself in friendly alignment with such pro-Hitler agitators as Fritz Kuhn, leader of the German-American Bund, and William D. Pelley, head of the Silver Shirts.

Brinkley even had ambitions of becoming the Republican presidential nominee in 1940, but things at last had begun going downhill for him. The Internal Revenue Service was trying to collect $200,000 in Brinkley's back income taxes. Former patients were filing malpractice suits that totaled millions. And Brinkley was confronted with competition in Del Rio from James R. Middlebrook, M.D., who advertised heavily over the air that he could do everything Brinkley could and at a lower price.

According to Carson, competition between Brinkley and Middlebrook became so intense that agents of both medics would board the Southern Pacific trains east and west of Del Rio in order to spot elderly passengers headed for Del Rio and switch them from Brinkley to Middlebrook or vice versa. Carson adds that "The railroad station platform at Del Rio was the last chance to rescue backsliders, and the pulling and hauling that went on there developed into gang fights on several occasions."

In part because of Middlebrook's competition and in part because of the malpractice suits, Brinkley abandoned Del Rio and set up a hospital in Little Rock, Arkansas. This new hospital went into receivership. Brinkley instituted personal bankruptcy proceedings in the hope of escaping payment of malpractice and tax claims, but he did so only after transferring most of his assets to his wife and son.

One of the last blows to befall him was the belated decision of the president of Mexico to honor that nation's commitment in the North American Regional Broadcasting Agreement of 1937 to delete XERA from the air. As Carson explains in his book,

Back in 1937 it had become front-page news when the North American Regional Broadcasting Agreement was signed at Havana, that the

Mexican mess would be straightened out. . . . Alas for reform . . . so skillful were the operators of these stations of nominal Mexican ownership in sabotaging the machinery of the cleanup that three years later the X-stations were still going strong. . . . Finally, when the President of Mexico was tipped off that the problem had a different dimension than United States discrimination against Mexicans, things began to happen. The American State Department and the Mexican Communications Ministry had fruitful conversations. . . . XERA was deleted from the official Mexican log of broadcasting stations effective March 29, 1941. On that date the radio voice of Dr. Brinkley was forever stilled.[7]

On March 29, 1941, XERA went silent.

John R. Brinkley died in Memphis, Tennessee, on May 26, 1942. The marble monument at his grave bears only this inscription: "J. R. Brinkley, M.D."

Norman Baker and His Cancer Cure

While Doc Brinkley was bilking the public in Kansas, Norman Baker was performing feats of medical prestidigitation in Muscatine, Iowa, with the aid of his own radio outlet, KTNT ("Know the Naked Truth"). Baker's broadcasts, which began in 1925, claimed to cure cancer, goiter, and appendicitis, all "without surgery or radium." For appendicitis he recommended application of a hot water bottle and "penetrating oil" to the painful spot.

Most of the material in this section is based on a chapter in *American Broadcasting* by Thomas W. Hoffer titled "TNT Baker: Radio Quack."[8] According to Hoffer, Baker denounced the use of aluminum cooking vessels as dangerous to health, as well as the tuberculin testing of cattle and smallpox immunization of school children. He attacked the American Medical Association as the "Medical Octopus" and claimed it had offered him a million dollars for his "cancer cure" so the cure could be suppressed and the public would have to resort to surgery. He launched attacks on the American Telephone and Telegraph Company, the Federal Radio Commission, and the publisher of the local newspaper, the *Muscatine Journal*.

In 1928 another applicant sought to obtain his radio frequency, citing public criticism of Baker's radio talks. A member of the FRC wrote Senator Smith Brookhart of Iowa that "most of our correspondence regarding this station is from Iowa listeners who say that its service is a disgrace and want it taken completely off the air." However, Hoffer says Brookhart intervened with the FRC on Baker's behalf, largely because KTNT had furnished free airtime to Brookhart, and for the time being Baker retained his license.

During the 1928 presidential campaign, Baker sold time to the Democratic National Committee to advocate the election of Al Smith. But Baker hated Smith and followed each pro-Smith broadcast with his own harangue urging the election of Herbert Hoover.

When the Democrats learned of this, they sent Baker this telegram: "MANY COMPLAINTS RECEIVED DEMOCRATIC NATIONAL COMMITTEE RE INTOLERANT RELIGIOUS PROPAGANDA EMANATING FROM YOUR STATION AGAINST SMITH. REPETITION OF SUCH SUBJECT MATTER GROUND FOR CANCELLATION REMAINING FARM NETWORK SCHEDULES." But Baker kept right on.

Baker had begun his career as a vaudeville hypnotist. Unlike Brinkley, he never claimed to be a doctor. He first took to the air over KTNT in 1925, promoting a number of his ventures including the Baker Institute (which he claimed could cure cancer), his daily newspaper, a mail-order house, auto service stations, and restaurants. His cancer cure and other enterprises netted Baker personal profits that rose to $1,700,000 in 1939.

Meanwhile, the redoubtable ex-vaudevillian had to surmount numerous roadblocks thrown up by unsympathetic state and federal authorities. He was convicted in Iowa of practicing medicine without a license, a problem he solved by leasing his Muscatine hospital to a licensed physician. Then late in 1930 the Federal Radio Commission voted to deny renewal of his license on grounds similar to those in the Brinkley case: Baker was using KTNT as a private mouthpiece rather than to serve the public interest. In February 1931 the Circuit Court of Appeals in Washington upheld the FRC's action. Baker gave his last broadcast on KTNT on June 12, 1931. He had tried, but failed, to get President Herbert Hoover to intercede on his behalf with the commission.

Like Brinkley, Baker had sued the American Medical Association for libel. But the AMA won by proving that the "cured" cancer patients whom Baker had been exhibiting either had died within five years or did not have cancer in the first place.

After losing his Iowa license Baker followed Brinkley's example by building a station in Mexico, this one in Nuevo Laredo, across the border from Baker's new headquarters in Laredo, Texas. Meanwhile, the attorney general of Iowa had learned that Baker still was in control of the Baker Institute at Muscatine despite his having "leased" it, and in 1932 got the Iowa Supreme Court to hold Baker in contempt and declare him a fugitive from justice. Proceedings were begun to extradite him from Texas, but Baker took refuge across the border at his Nuevo Laredo station, then under construction. It was scheduled to start with a power of 75 kilowatts (25 more than any station in the United States) and ultimately go up to 750 kilowatts.

Baker announced that his new station, XENT, would campaign against Herbert Hoover during the 1932 campaign because Hoover had refused to intervene with the FRC on his behalf. The Hoover administration reacted by trying to persuade the Mexican government to delay the opening of the new station until after the November election. Mexico refused, but Baker encountered so many technical problems in getting the station on the air that it did not begin broadcasting until October 1933. It never succeeded in getting its power above the original 75 kilowatts and was heard only at night, but its post-sunset signal reached far north and enabled Baker to advertise his new hospital in Laredo, as well as his plans for another in Eureka Springs, Arkansas.

Meanwhile, Congress became concerned about the growing number of stations across the border that were beaming English-language programs to this country to advertise quack remedies and far-out political philosophies. It enacted Section 325(b) of the Communications Act. This prohibited the use in this country of radio studios, telephone lines, or recording apparatus for the preparation or transmission of programs for stations in foreign countries powerful enough to be heard in the United States, unless the permission of the FCC was obtained. Criminal proceedings under this statute ultimately were begun against Baker in 1937, and he was convicted in federal district court, but the conviction was reversed by the Fifth Circuit Court of Appeals in one of the most puzzling decisions ever handed down. In effect, the court said that despite the clear language and obvious intent of the statute it did not "prohibit the recordation of sound waves in the United States and sending the record to Mexico to have the sound waves there reproduced and broadcast." Of course, this was exactly what Baker and Brinkley were doing, and Congress was trying to stop.

Like Brinkley, Baker had political ambitions. He ran for nomination to the U.S. Senate in the 1936 Iowa Republican primary but was fourth in a field of six. His broadcasts, like Brinkley's, eventually took on an anti-Semitic tone. He accused Jewish doctors of denying him recognition for his cancer cure and professed to believe that "the Jews are killing people by their claiming to have a cure for cancer, and all of them ought to be taken back to Germany and let Hitler do with them what he wants to."[9]

Meanwhile, Baker had completed his new hospital in Eureka Springs, Arkansas, and moved his headquarters there, still recording his programs for broadcast over XENT in Nuevo Laredo.

His career had passed its zenith, however. Federal authorities charged him with using the mails to defraud. He was tried in Little Rock, Arkansas, in 1940 and sentenced to four years imprisonment. The Baker hospitals closed, but XENT stayed on the air, operated by a trusted employee, Thelma Yount, until 1944, when the Mexican government finally heeded Washington's requests and took the station off the air.

After Baker got out of prison in 1944, he retired to his yacht in Florida and left broadcasting behind.

Thus, our government ultimately was able to silence both of the medical quacks described in this chapter, but the Federal Communications Commission never again has tried to enforce Section 325(b) of the Communications Act because of the strange decision of the Fifth Circuit Court of Appeals. English-language stations in Tijuana and other Mexican cities still transmit programs across the border that have been recorded for that purpose in this country.

6

The Radio Preachers

TO SECRETARY OF COMMERCE HERBERT HOOVER:

PLEASE ORDER YOUR MINIONS OF SATAN TO LEAVE MY STATION ALONE. STOP. YOU CANNOT EXPECT THE ALMIGHTY TO ABIDE BY YOUR WAVE LENGTH NONSENSE. STOP. WHEN I OFFER MY PRAYERS TO HIM I MUST FIT INTO HIS RECEPTION. STOP. OPEN THE STATION AT ONCE. STOP.

AIMEE SEMPLE McPHERSON

Medical quacks plagued radio regulators in the early days of broadcasting, but radio preachers have caused considerably more problems, perhaps because they are not subject to government regulation in their calling, whereas physicians must at least be licensed.

Some of the radio preachers have been out-and-out frauds, peddling tips on the local numbers game in the guise of citing chapter and verse from the Bible or selling anointed prayer cloths and other paraphernalia guaranteed to assure financial blessings, good health, and a satisfactory love life.

Then there are today's television evangelists such as Jim Bakker with his PTL ministry, Oral Roberts and his threats that God would snatch him up to heaven unless millions in contributions were quickly forthcoming, and Jimmy Swaggart, tearfully confessing his sin.

This chapter tells how the FCC whitewashed the case of Jim Bakker, despite overwhelming evidence that he was violating a federal criminal statute by misappropriating millions of dollars.

One of the high points of early religious advertising was reached by a Wheeling, West Virginia, station years ago when it broadcast offers to sell "an autographed picture of John the Baptist" for one dollar.

Among the first to discover the power of radio to spread one's own version of the True Word were a quartet of dissimilar divines who took to the air in the 1920s. Two—Aimee Semple McPherson and Robert Shuler—thrived in that hothouse of religious fanaticism, Los Angeles. The other two broadcast from the Middle West. One was the Reverend Charles E. Coughlin of Royal Oak, Michigan; the other, Wilbur Glen Voliva, chief apostle of the Christian Catholic Apostolic Church of Zion, Illinois.

Aimee Semple McPherson

Aimee McPherson was a flamboyant female evangelist who preached what she called the Four Square Gospel in her Angelus Temple in Los Angeles. Her radio station, KFSG ("Kall Four Square Gospel"), broadcast her sermons.

Before the Federal Radio Commission was established in 1927, the secretary of commerce, then Herbert Hoover, was responsible for regulating radio stations to the extent to which they were subject to regulation under the outdated Radio Act of 1912. Hoover issued licenses to stations, which specified their locations, wavelengths, and operating power. One station that kept straying from its assigned wavelength was McPherson's KFSG. After many warnings, Hoover ordered it off the air and promptly received the telegram that heads this chapter.[1] The station later was allowed to resume broadcasting and remained under the ownership of the church until sold many years later.

"Fighting Bob" Shuler

One of the landmark cases in radio regulation under the Federal Radio Commission involved a Los Angeles station used by a minister from 1926 to 1932 to broadcast scandalous personal attacks on public figures. The station was KGEF, licensed to Trinity Methodist Church, South. Its minister was a firebrand named Robert "Fighting Bob" Shuler, who used KGEF to attack, among other institutions and persons, the Roman Catholic Church, the local courts, and specific judges whom he charged with sundry immoral acts.[2]

Shuler twice was held in contempt of court because of his comments on current cases, and he once spent two weeks in jail as punishment. During the trials of movie magnate Alexander Pantages and his wife, Shuler alleged that their wealth was being used for jury fixing. Then he broadcast comments on the alleged drinking habits and extramarital activities of one particular juror. After this, it was said in Los Angeles that juries always convicted Shuler's enemies for fear of what he might broadcast about them.

When Shuler first went to Trinity Church from the backwoods of Texas, the church had only 900 members and was seventy thousand dollars in debt according to a December 1931 article in the *New Republic* by Edmund Wilson. In ten years membership grew to 42,000, and Shuler was the most powerful person in the city. The principal reason for this change was his acquisition of KGEF. The station was given to him by a wealthy spinster admirer, and he promptly began to use it to air scandal. The first major expose concerned the Los Angeles police chief's relations with another man's wife. The chief was fired.

Among Shuler's accomplishments during his heyday were

• Helping to send District Attorney Asa M. Keyes to San Quentin prison for taking bribes
• Getting an ex-Klansman elected mayor of Los Angeles and compelling him to fire the police chief. (Shuler broadcast,

"I don't *say* that I believe these perverted practices on the part of
Chief Davis," but added that he did believe that the chief was
allied with bootleggers, gamblers, and brothelkeepers)
  • Denouncing the powerful publisher, William Randolph
Hearst, and his mistress, Actress Marion Davies
  • Attacking the Knights of Columbus, which unsuccess-
fully sued him twice for libel.

Shuler even attacked his fellow cleric, Aimee McPherson,
but the peak of his performance may have been reached when,
as the U.S. Court of Appeals later put it, "on one occasion he
announced over the radio that he had certain damaging information against a prominent unnamed man, which, unless a contribution (presumably to the church) of $100 was forthcoming,
he would disclose. As a result, he received contributions from
several persons."[3]
According to the *New Republic* article, an anonymous admirer in Pasadena supplied him with a private detective to aid in
ferreting out the information he exposed. Later another admirer
set him up with a whole corps of spies. His power burgeoned.
"He broke a district attorney, a city prosecutor and two police
chiefs. Politicians played up to him. Newspapers and juries
came to fear him. No sin was too unseemly or intimate for him
to make known."
Finally, after receiving many complaints against Shuler, the
Federal Radio Commission in 1931 refused to renew the station
license on the grounds that "the public interest, convenience and
necessity" were not being served by its broadcasts. The commission believed them to be "sensational rather than instructive."
The Circuit Court of Appeals upheld the decision. It found that
Shuler had used the station to "obstruct the administration of
justice, offend the religious susceptibilities of thousands, inspire
political distrust and civic discord [and] offend youth and inno-
cence by free use of words suggestive of sexual immorality."[4]
(Shuler had at times referred to "pimps" and "prostitutes.")
The U.S. Supreme Court declined to review the lower court
decision, and KGEF was banished from the air.
This case often has been cited as precedent for the commis-

sion's right to consider program content in reviewing licenses, even though the Communications Act forbids censorship of program matter.

However, Federal Communications Commissions of later years would not have taken away a station's license on the cited grounds in the Shuler case because of the no-censorship provision of the statute and the First Amendment guaranties of freedom of speech and press. A modern commission might have imposed some sort of sanction on Shuler for violation of the fairness doctrine or personal attack rule, but if he offered to permit presentation of contrasting views on controversial issues or gave persons who were attacked a chance to respond, he would be safe, no matter how violent his diatribes. The phrase "public interest, convenience and necessity" sets such a vague standard that modern commissions have been chary of revoking station licenses on this ground alone. Otherwise, any broadcast that happened to offend a current majority of the commission might be found to be contrary to the public interest. The courts likewise now are more concerned than they were in 1931 over infringement of free speech guaranties, and they would reverse any such action by the commission.

Father Coughlin

Politically, the most influential of the microphone ministers was Father Charles E. Coughlin, a Catholic parish priest in Royal Oak, Michigan, near Detroit. Coughlin began delivering radio sermons over a local station in 1926 but did not turn to politics until late 1930, after the Great Depression had set in. Then he began denouncing money changers and jumped on the Roosevelt bandwagon in 1932, proclaiming "Roosevelt or Ruin." His "Golden Hour" was picked up by the CBS radio network. After CBS dropped his increasingly controversial broadcasts, he formed an independent network that grew to fifty-eight stations.[5]

When Roosevelt was elected president, Coughlin apparently expected to be taken into FDR's inner circle of advisers, but Roosevelt carefully kept his distance. In anger, Coughlin turned against Roosevelt. Supported by his bishop, he founded what he called the National Union for Social Justice and, as the 1936 presidential campaign approached, formed his own "Union" political party. Congressman William Lemke of North Dakota was its candidate for president. Coughlin claimed he would deliver ten million votes, but Lemke drew less than one-tenth of that number.

A new bishop assumed office in 1937 and Coughlin began to encounter trouble, but he was not to be deterred. His broadcasts became increasingly anti-Semitic and pro-Nazi. He repeatedly attacked what he called "godless Jews," although he denied being anti-Semitic. He was against only *godless* Jews!

In 1939 he urged listeners to organize an "army of peace" and march on Washington to protest the liberalization of the neutrality laws. His tirades were offensive to many Catholics including George Cardinal Mundelein of Chicago. Mundelein once became so outraged over a Coughlin broadcast that he called the top brass at NBC one Sunday and obtained a half-hour of network time to be used that afternoon. Then he sent his chief aide, Auxiliary Bishop Bernard J. Sheil, to the NBC Chicago studios to deliver a reply to Coughlin's broadcast.

As Coughlin became more violent, more and more stations became leery of carrying his broadcasts. In 1939 the Code Committee of the National Association of Broadcasters decided that discussion of American neutrality on sponsored programs was controversial and hence violated the code. More stations canceled Coughlin's broadcasts.

His church superiors finally silenced him.[6]

"The Earth Is Flat"

A major early case in which a principal issue was material broadcast by a preacher was the celebrated Great Lakes Broadcasting Company case, already mentioned in Chapters 2 and 4.

The meaning of the radio commission's decision was to be distorted for partisan political purposes by the FCC more than thirty years later.

When the first radio stations were licensed in the early 1920s, only a few frequencies were set aside for broadcast purposes, and two or more stations in the same area often had to divide time on the same frequency. Three time-sharers in the Chicago area were WLS, which had been founded by Sears Roebuck & Company (hence the call letters, standing for "World's Largest Store"); WENR, another Chicago station that later was consolidated with WLS to form ABC's full-time AM station in Chicago; and WCBD, owned by the Christian Catholic Apostolic Church, which operated a communal village named Zion on the shores of Lake Michigan forty miles north of Chicago.

Each of the stations asked the radio commission to increase its share of the broadcast day. WENR and WLS were standard commercial stations, except that WLS emphasized farm programming. WCBD was used by the head of the Christian Catholic Apostolic Church, Wilbur Glen Voliva, to advance the unusual religious tenets of that tiny sect—one being that the earth was flat and surrounded by a wall of clear ice.

The Federal Radio Commission voted to reduce the share of time allocated to Voliva's WCBD. The reason, it said, was that a station was licensed to serve the public in general, not merely the members of one small religious sect.

The conclusion is unavoidable that this station [WCBD] in emphasis is operated for the purpose of propagating the creed of its owner. . . . The members of the faith and of the persons interested in it are extremely limited in number compared with those of other faiths, and it is not logical that such a sect should enjoy peculiar facilities for propagating its beliefs when there is not room in the ether for the many other sects to have their separate stations.[7]

Although the FRC's decision to reduce WCBD's share of the broadcast day had only minor local consequences, it became a major precedent in broadcast regulation. As explained in Chapter 4, the commission's language in this case became the foundation for the later-enunciated fairness doctrine. And, as explained in Chapter 2, one part of the 1929 Great Lakes ruling was distorted by the Federal Communications Commission twenty-five years later to justify the award of a license that actually was based on political favoritism.

Biblical Tips on the Numbers Game—
WOOK and WIGO

Perhaps the most blatant misuse of broadcast time in the name of religion has been by a number of "ministers" who have made a wide assortment of false promises including claims of predicting winning combinations of numerals in the numbers game, an illegal lottery that flourishes chiefly among low-income persons, including a large proportion of blacks.

Bogus biblical tips on the numbers racket were broadcast on black-oriented stations for years, but none lost its license on this ground until 1975, when station WOOK in Washington, D.C., was denied renewal.[8]

At renewal time any person may file an application for an existing station's license, citing reasons why the new applicant would serve "the public interest, convenience and necessity" better than the incumbent licensee. When another applicant challenged WOOK's renewal, its charges against the incumbent licensee were based in part on the so-called religious broadcasts of the station and the fact that they consisted mainly of three-digit scriptural citations that were tips on the local numbers game. This violated two laws. It was false advertising, since the ministers could not, as they claimed, accurately forecast winning numbers. It also violated federal laws that prohibited the broadcast of information about a lottery.

Perhaps an explanation is due of how the numbers game works. Players may bet any amount from twenty-five cents up on each day's game. The winning number consists of three digits and is based either on the pari-mutuel prices paid later that day at a specified horse track or on the volume of stocks transferred on the New York Stock Exchange. Since any one of 999 numbers may be a winner, the odds against winning a three-digit bet are 998 to 1. The actual payoff is much less, perhaps five hundred to one, and varies from city to city. The difference represents the profit of the operator and his or her expenses, which in many cities include bribes to police. A player also may bet on two-digit combinations or even on whether a single digit will be the first, middle, or last one of a winning number. The payoff for these bets is much less than for "hitting" a three-digit number.

Here is some of the evidence cited by the hearing examiner in his decision in the WOOK case.

Queen Mother Ruby Etta Allen, an itinerant minister, . . . broadcast her program "Showers of Blessing" over WOOK in which she offered a "Seven Day Blessing Plan" for a donation of $10.50. In her broadcast it was represented that during her first week in Washington, D.C., God blessed the people three times from the blessing plan and through her blessing plan had on Monday blessed "on the 25th Psalm" and on "Psalm 71 and 9" on Tuesday. The winning numbers in the numbers game on Monday and Tuesday of the preceding week were 250 and 719.[9]

The claims of having predicted winning numbers were false. They apparently were based on the assumption that most listeners did not know of the biblical citations previously broadcast.

Another excerpt from the initial decision:

On February 16, 1969, Reverend J. Williams, an itinerant minister . . . represented that he brought a "money blessing" the previous week . . . and that "I blessed last week on Monday, Tuesday and Friday. . . . I told children to ask God for $953; I told them to ask God for $905; and I told them to ask Him for $301 and oh you were blessed honestly three times last week." He further represented that "I'm going to do the same for you this week here in Washington. . . . I guarantee it. . . . I'm going to give you a bank account. I'm going to give you a home. I'm going to give you a car. Whatever you need . . . I have your answer." The winning numbers in the numbers game on Monday and Tuesday of the previous week were 953 and 905. The winning number for Friday was 351 rather than 301, this having been the winning number of Wednesday.[10]

The FCC decision taking away WOOK's license in 1975 also referred to offers of "roots," "incense," and "spiritual baths" as means of attaining financial gain or solving personal problems. WOOK claimed that "the sale of these items was not unlike the sale of a rosary and that the articles were intended to bring the audience of the radio ministers closer to God," but the FCC concluded that "the representations which accompanied the offers of these articles were without religious or factual basis."[11]

An example of the moral principles advocated by some of WOOK's radio ministers was supplied by Bishop Bonner. In imploring his listeners to come to his Washington headquarters to obtain the benefits of his "money-drawing root" and "very special money-drawing incense," the Bishop urged:

Starting at 7 A.M. before you go to work Monday morning come by. If you have to take off, take off. Don't go to work Monday morning. If you got to be late, call and say I've got to go to the doctor. I'm sick. The baby fell down the steps. Grandmother took sick. Just anything happened, but come by 1443 G Street, N.E., before you go to work on tomorrow morning.[12]

Six years after it denied license renewal to WOOK in 1975, the commission refused to impose the same penalty on another station that broadcast the same type of programming.

The second offender was WIGO, a black-oriented station in Atlanta with an absentee owner in New York. Maynard Jackson, mayor of Atlanta, first brought the station's programming to official attention after he chanced to hear one of its Sunday "religious" programs. The commission conducted an investigation and then issued an order to show cause why the license of WIGO should not be revoked. The order provided for a possible alternative sanction of a ten thousand dollar forfeiture.

Administrative Law Judge John Conlin's initial decision in the case was to revoke the WIGO license. The members of the commission, however, took a more tolerant attitude toward fraudulent religious broadcasts than they had before. Although

WIGO was selling time to fake ministers at a rate of $170,000 per year, the FCC in January 1981 voted to fine the licensee, WIGO, Inc., ten thousand dollars rather than to revoke his license.[13]

The commission talked out of both sides of its mouth in the decision. It said (1) the broadcasts clearly promoted a lottery, and (2) the station manager knew, or should have known, that fake lottery forecasts were being broadcast, since members of his staff had told him so and a local newspaper had published the fact that one of the WIGO "ministers" had been convicted of a gambling charge stemming from his broadcasts.

But the commission found two reasons to favor the licensee: (1) although the absentee owner was legally responsible for the misconduct at the station he was "not *grossly* negligent" [emphasis added]; (2) the station's overall programming was "meritorious."[14]

The FCC had to tread a narrow path on the issue of the absentee owner's responsibility for the illegal programming. It had often held that licensees would not be excused on the grounds that they were absentee owners and didn't know what was going on at their stations. In the WIGO case the owner came down from New York only one day a month to "supervise" the operation of the station and claimed that he never had listened to any of the religious broadcasts that supplied a large part of his revenue. It must have been difficult for the commission to escape the conclusion that if the owner had not bothered to learn any more than this about his programming, he had not supervised the station adequately and should lose his license on that basis, like other owners who had been denied renewal in the past.

The commission's other reason for not revoking the license was that WIGO's programming was "meritorious." Attorneys for stations that are in danger of losing their licenses almost always petition the FCC to add a "meritorious programming" issue to those already designated for resolution in the forthcoming hearing. Then they introduce voluminous exhibits to bolster their contention in mitigation of the licensee's sins that the FCC should take into consideration the worthwhile programming that the station has broadcast in other parts of its schedule.

The attorneys in the Broadcast Bureau's Hearing Division, who act as prosecuting attorneys after the commission orders a hearing on renewal or revocation of a license, have neither the time nor the resources to undertake the arduous task of gathering evidence to counter a licensee's claims of having broadcast "meritorious" programming. Thus, that part of a licensee's defense always goes unanswered.

It has always seemed to me that excusing major violations on the ground that a station has broadcast some meritorious programming is equivalent to acquitting Adolf Hitler because he was good to his mother. Under the Communications Act, all stations are required to present meritorious programming. In addition, they are required to abide by the law, and the FCC is authorized to revoke their licenses for violations of certain statutes including those that prohibit use of radio to promote illegal lotteries and to obtain money under false pretenses, both of which were violated by WIGO.

Why such different outcomes of the WOOK and WIGO cases? Perhaps administrative leadership made a difference. The WOOK decision came in 1975 when the commission was headed by an outstanding chairman, Richard E. Wiley. Although definitely probusiness, he believed in enforcing the law. The WIGO decision came in January 1981, when the commission was drifting along under a lame duck chairman, Charles Ferris, pending the arrival of Reagan's appointee, Mark Fowler.

The FCC Lets Jim Bakker off the Hook

In what may have been the most disgraceful decision in FCC history, the commission in 1982 brushed what it had discovered about Evangelist Jim Bakker under the carpet and let him continue to bilk his TV followers of millions of dollars for five more years until a sexual adventure led to his exposure.

The commission's actions in the Bakker case were made all the more flagrant by the contrast between it and a previous one involving similar allegations, which had resulted in a minister's losing his TV license. Briefly, the facts of the first case were these.

KHOF-TV, San Bernardino, California, was licensed to Faith Center, Inc., which was headed by the Reverend W. Eugene Scott. Former employees of KHOF complained to the commission that the station was soliciting contributions for certain announced purposes but spending the money for others. The FCC sent investigators to the station. Scott refused to produce financial or program records, videotapes of the programs in question, or any other records, although the commission has authority under the Communications Act to investigate its licensees. Scott claimed that he was protected by the freedom of religion clause of the First Amendment.

The FCC informed him that the First Amendment did not bar it from investigating charges that he had been violating Section 1343 of the U.S. Criminal Code.[15] When Scott continued to deny access to station records, the commission designated the renewal application of the station for hearing and ultimately took away the license.[16]

The result was entirely different when the same charges were later made against WJAN-TV, Canton, Ohio, which was licensed to a subsidiary of Bakker's PTL (Praise the Lord) television network. When commission investigators went to that station in March 1979 they were denied an opportunity to interview its officers and employees or to obtain the station's financial records or recordings of the programs on which funds had been solicited.

As it had in the Scott case, the commission ordered the licensee to make its records and personnel available. The licensee refused. The FCC then voted to hold a nonpublic, formal inquiry under Section 403 of the Communications Act, so that records could be subpoenaed and officers and employees compelled to testify under oath. Attorney Lawrence Bernstein of the Broadcast Bureau was assigned to conduct the inquiry. However, at the end of the proceeding the commission neither voted to hold a public renewal hearing nor issued any statement as to what its inquiry had revealed. Instead, it announced in a thirteen-line press release that the licensee was being allowed to sell the station to another religious organization and that the FCC had ordered its staff to forward "relevant information" about the nonpublic inquiry to the Department of Justice.[17]

Thus did the commission avoid disclosure of the damning facts Bernstein had unearthed during the nonpublic hearing, and let Bakker go free. Although four of the seven commissioners chose to refer the case to the Justice Department, they well knew that Section 312(a)(6) of the Communications Act explicitly authorizes the FCC itself to take action for violation of Section 1343 by revoking the station's license. In previous cases the commission acting under this section had made its own decision whether to revoke or refuse to renew the station's license.

The decision of the commission still left the Justice Department free to bring criminal charges against the licensee, regardless of what the FCC had done. But, as we shall see, President Reagan's Justice Department was no more inclined than was his communications commission to take action against fundamentalist television preachers.

The action of the FCC majority caused two of the three dissenting commissioners, Joseph R. Fogarty and Henry M. Rivera, to issue one of the bitterest dissents on record. In part, it read,

[T]he majority's action is contrary to our established broadcast licensing law and policy, wholly unexplained on any public record, and prejudicial to the credibility of this Commission's enforcement responsibilities. . . . It is plain that the record [of the nonpublic inquiry] raises substantial and material questions as to whether PTL engaged in fraudulent solicitation of funds over the air, whether it breached its fiduciary duty, whether the President and Chairman of the Board of PTL gave false testimony to the Commission, and whether witnesses before the Commission were corruptly influenced.[18]

The dissent pointed out that with the exception of a few circumstances not present in the WJAN case, the commission in the past had refused to allow stations to sell their licenses until the FCC first had determined whether the licensee still had a license to sell.

The dissent ended with these words.

Based on fact, law and policy, PTL should be designated for hearing on the serious misconduct issues raised by the Commission's Section 403 investigation. The majority has short-circuited proper process with no explanation, thereby clearly signifying its lack of courage of whatever convictions may have led it to this malodorous result. Lacking official notice of the basis for this action, we dissent from the stench.[19]

In addition to its strange outcome, another unusual circumstance in this case was cited in the dissent. The first attempt to obtain a commission vote on the case was made on July 26, 1982, by means of a "circulation vote." That is, instead of scheduling the case for a commission meeting where discussion could take place, Chairman Mark Fowler sent the general counsel – at that time Stephen A. Sharp – around to each commissioner's office in an effort to obtain approval via the circulation method. When this is done, a copy of a proposed commission decision is taken to each commissioner's office with a ballot on which he or she may vote for or against it. A proposed commission action normally is handled in this way only if it involves a routine, noncontroversial matter or if it is so urgent that it cannot await the next commission meeting. When an item is presented by the circulation method, a commissioner usually does not know the views of colleagues, has no opportunity to base a judgment on the discussion at a commission meeting, and has no opportunity to question members of the staff who handled the case.

The item that Sharp carried to the commissioners' offices on July 26, 1982, fell into neither of the two circulation-vote categories. The proposed action was not routine; it was unprecedented and highly controversial. And it was not so urgent that it required an immediate vote. This was made clear by the subsequent history of the proposal. After some commissioners objected to the effort to ram the proposal through on July 26, the item was withdrawn and was not brought back for consideration until the commission meeting of December 8, 1982.

The long delay may have been caused by Fowler's realization that the proposal could not muster a four-member majority. During the interval between July 26 and December 8, Sharp was appointed a commissioner. On December 8 he cast the deciding vote for approval.

The most unfortunate consequence of the PTL decision did not become apparent until almost five years later, when the Pearlygate scandal hit the headlines and James O. Bakker, president of both PTL and WJAN-TV, was exposed as having been involved in sexual misconduct with Jessica Hahn. Later Hahn was paid $265,000 in hush money out of PTL funds. This led to a series of further revelations about Bakker and his wife, Tammy. It was learned that with money contributed by the faithful to the cause of God, they had built themselves six luxurious homes, some with gold-plated bathroom fixtures and, at one, an air-conditioned doghouse. The Bakkers also had paid themselves $1,600,000 in salaries and bonuses in 1986. In addition, they had used PTL expense-account money for many personal purposes, ranging from tutors for their children to repair of their home lawn-sprinkler systems.[20]

The president of PTL and of the corporate licensee of WJAN-TV were the same—James O. Bakker. Thus, it was Bakker to whom Commissioners Fogarty and Rivera referred in their dissent when they stated that the record of the nonpublic inquiry raised "substantial and material questions as to whether PTL engaged in fraudulent solicitation of funds over the air [and] *whether the President and Chairman of the Board of PTL gave false testimony to the Commission, and whether witnesses before the Commission were corruptly influenced*" [emphasis added].

Had the FCC majority not whitewashed the case, the truth about Bakker's television ministry probably would have been exposed years earlier, and misguided contributors might have been saved millions of dollars.

The commission's conduct in the PTL case was so scandalous that the Public Broadcasting System (PBS) TV network produced an hour-long documentary program, "Praise the Lord," which was mainly devoted to it. Among the facts dug up by Scott Malone, investigative reporter for the PBS Front Line series, were these: (1) Attorney Lawrence Bernstein's report to the commission on what the inquiry had revealed was allowed to languish for almost two years and was rewritten three times before it was made available to members of the commission; (2) while the report was in the office of Stephen Sharp, general counsel, 134 sections were deleted between the third and fourth drafts alone, as well as thirty-six source references that gave specific examples of Bakker's fraud and perjury; and (3) Bakker himself was on the witness stand eleven days. FCC transcripts of his testimony and other written evidence reveal that his statements under oath were contradicted by other witnesses twenty-seven times, by his own testimony thirty-six times, and by other evidence eighty-one times. Bernstein says these figures are conservative, since they were based only on the third and fourth drafts of his report, which were the only ones PBS was able to obtain.

Sharp blandly denied on the program that he had made any changes in the report except editorial ones, although he admitted that he was "not pleased" with the report. Ex-chairman Fowler also denied making changes. Although Fowler was having commission meetings videotaped by that time, he refused to release tapes of the closed meeting at which the final vote in this case was taken.

Ex-commissioner Anne Jones, one of the three who dissented, says she didn't know the report had been altered. Ex-commissioner Mimi Weyforth Dawson, who reportedly was silent during the meeting but later voted with Fowler, Sharp, and James Quello, refused a PBS request for an interview.

During the pendency of the case before the FCC, Bakker made financial hay by pleading on the air for contributions to "protect the cause of American religion." He accused the commission of being in league with the devil. All told, he raised twenty-two million dollars for the announced purpose of defending the faith against the FCC.

Attorney Bernstein, for years an able and loyal member of the FCC staff, quit the commission in disgust early in 1983. The most shocking thing about the commission's conduct in this case, he thinks, was its failure to exercise its responsibility to protect the American people. He told me, "After the FCC refused to do anything against him, Bakker got the idea that he was untouchable and began appropriating more and more millions." (PTL revenues rose from 28 million dollars in 1978 to 129 million in 1986. Jim and Tammy's personal income ballooned proportionately.)

Two other major branches of the Reagan administration were as disinclined as the FCC to take any action that might alienate one of television's most widely followed fundamentalist preachers—a group that was expected to back Reagan in his 1984 reelection bid.

The Internal Revenue Service began an inquiry into PTL finances in 1981 but dragged its feet until the Bakker scandal broke in the press. Finally, on April 22, 1988, the IRS announced that it had revoked PTL's tax-exempt status.

The Justice Department, to which the commission had referred the case, announced shortly thereafter that it had no intention of launching criminal prosecution. As the PBS documentary revealed, Charles Brewer, the U.S. attorney based in Asheville, North Carolina, had proposed an investigation of PTL, but as soon as Washington headquarters got word of his intentions, he was called there by Deputy Attorney General Arnold Burns to attend a meeting on the subject. Also present at the meeting were two Justice Department attorneys who opposed beginning any investigation, Vinton Lide, U.S. attorney in Columbia, South Carolina, and Michael Durney. Soon thereafter, the PTL case was taken away from Brewer and turned over to the two attorneys who wanted to drop it!

The Reverend Carl McIntire and WXUR

The commission encountered problems with an entirely different kind of religious programming in the early 1960s. Stations WXUR and WXUR-FM, Media, Pennsylvania, were owned by Faith Theological Seminary, whose board chairman was the Reverend Carl McIntire. McIntire also was pastor of the Bible Presbyterian Church of Collingswood, New Jersey, and he held effective control of Sheldon College, the *Christian Beacon* magazine, the Christian Admiral Hotel of Cape May, New Jersey, and the American and International Councils of Christian Churches.

He was best known nationally for his daily program, the "Twentieth Century Reformation Hour" (actually only thirty minutes long). His sidekick on the program was an aide whom he called "Amen Charlie." Charlie's function seemed to be to utter an occasional "Amen" to McIntire's fulminations against his enemies and sin in general.

McIntire had been ordained a minister of the United Presbyterian Church but had parted company with it because he thought it too liberal, theologically and otherwise. Later, because of his antagonism toward the National and World Councils of Churches, he established the American Council of Churches and the International Council of Churches. He used his "Reformation Hour" to attack prominent persons and organizations for a variety of alleged sins, including "liberalism, modernism, socialism and communism." In so doing he eventually ran afoul of the fairness doctrine and the commission's personal attack policy.

The fairness doctrine requires a station whose broadcasts advocate one side of a controversial public issue to "afford reasonable opportunity for presentation of contrasting views" on the issue. If discussion of such an issue includes an attack on the character, honesty, or integrity of someone, the station must send that person a copy of the attack and an offer of airtime for a reply. The responsibility for complying with these requirements rests with the station. (See Chapter 4.)

The FCC began getting complaints that the stations broadcasting the McIntire program were not complying with the fairness doctrine or the personal attack policy. When queried by the commission, most station owners replied that they received the tape recordings of the program unaccompanied by scripts, and they usually didn't listen to the tapes before broadcasting them. The FCC told them it was their responsibility to learn what they were about to broadcast. McIntire flew into a rage at what he charged was interference with his right to freedom of speech. On one of his broadcasts, he said he ad-libbed his program without benefit of scripts and often he didn't know when he began a program what he was going to say on it. So how was he to furnish scripts to his stations? It was all a plot to force him off the air.

Some stations cancelled the program because they thought it would be too much trouble to preaudition the daily tapes and to invite other persons to broadcast contrasting views or respond to personal attacks. McIntire appealed to Congress to halt this diabolical FCC plot. He got himself invited to testify before congressional committees, staged marches on the streets of Washington, picketed the FCC building, and even gathered with some of his followers outside the office of the FCC chairman, Rosel Hyde, where they knelt and prayed that Hyde (who was a devout Mormon) might be enlightened and relieve them of their burden.

One of the stations that cancelled the program was in Chester, Pennsylvania. It had been McIntire's outlet in the Philadelphia area. He learned at about the same time that WXUR-AM and FM in Media, Pennsylvania, were for sale. Since these stations also could reach the Philadelphia audience, he arranged for the Faith Theological Seminary to buy them and filed an application with the FCC for approval of the sale.

Protests were filed with the FCC immediately by many organizations including the NAACP, the National Urban League, the Anti-Defamation League of B'nai B'rith, the AFL-CIO, the United Church of Christ, and the regional organizations of the Presbyterian, Baptist, Lutheran, and Catholic churches. Their complaint was that McIntire would control the stations and that in his nationally syndicated program he had distorted facts on issues such as race relations, religious unity, and foreign aid. They also stated that he had made

intemperate attacks on other religious denominations and leaders . . . governmental agencies, political figures and international organizations . . . and that in light of his record of partisan and extremist views, he lacked the degree of public and social responsibility demanded of broadcast licensees, and that these views would carry over into the operation of the stations.

In response Faith Seminary promised "to make time available on an equal and non-discriminatory basis to all religious faiths requesting time" and to afford equal opportunities to opposing views on controversial public issues.

The FCC approved the sale of WXUR to the McIntire organization but in doing so called that group's attention to the fairness doctrine and personal attack policy and said it would be expected "to operate in accordance with these requirements." As if still dubious about the whole thing, it added a final warning: "In reaching this determination we have relied upon the specific representations of the transferee [buyer] indicating awareness of the licensee's responsibilities. In any event, this grant is subject to the same conditions applicable to all broadcast grants," which, it said, included abiding by the fairness doctrine.

It was not long before the FCC began receiving complaints that the new licensee was violating its promises — that it was not making "time available on an equal and non-discriminatory basis to all religious faiths" and that it was violating the fairness doctrine and the personal attack principle. The Pennsylvania House of Representatives joined the chorus of protests.

Before Newton Minow became its chairman in 1961, the Federal Communications Commission had done little to enforce the fairness doctrine except, as an October 1961 *George Washington University Law Review* article stated, to "issue pious admonitions" to violators. Under Minow, however, the FCC began an active effort to enforce this as well as other laws and policies. WXUR appeared to be as sound a case as the commission was likely to find in which to make clear its determination to enforce the fairness doctrine. In 1963 an investigation was launched, which included recording WXUR's entire program schedule of eleven hours per day for fifteen days.

After a long and acrimonious hearing, the FCC voted in July 1970 to deny the renewal application of WXUR and WXUR-FM. The decision pointed out the station's failure to keep its earlier promise.

The record demonstrates that [WXUR] failed to provide reasonable opportunities for the presentation of contrasting views on controversial issues of public importance, that it ignored the personal attack principle of the Fairness Doctrine, that the applicant's representations as to the manner in which the station would be operated were not adhered to. . . . Any one of these violations would alone be sufficient to require denying the renewals here, and the violations are rendered even more serious by the fact that we carefully drew the [Faith Theological] Seminary's attention to a licensee's responsibilities before we approved transfer of the stations to its ownership and control.[21]

The U.S. Circuit Court of Appeals affirmed the decision by a two-to-one vote in September 1972.[21] Although all three judges found that the stations had violated the fairness doctrine and the personal attack principle many times, two of them were unwilling to deny license renewal on this basis. However, the majority affirmed the commission on the grounds that the licensee had misrepresented its program plans in its application to buy the stations, and "thus consciously deceived the Commission." The court minced no words in condemning Faith Seminary. The licensee's record was "bleak in the areas of good faith." Its actions showed "a common design to engage in deceit and trickery in obtaining a broadcast license" and it had "blazed a trail marked by empty promises and valueless verbiage." WXUR-AM and FM went off the air in July 1973.

Thereupon, McIntire announced that in order to preserve freedom of speech, he would establish a station on a ship off the Atlantic Coast. He made good on his threat for a short time in September 1973 by operating a station aboard a converted World War II minesweeper off Cape May, New Jersey. He called it "Radio Free America." It is believed to have been the first "pirate" station to operate off the American coast, although illegal stations had broadcast from time to time from ships in the North Sea until captured and silenced by the navies of Britain and northern European countries.

Two days after McIntire began broadcasting from the ship, attorneys for the FCC and the Justice Department obtained an order from a federal district court directing the unlicensed station to cease operation. On October 25, 1973, the judge denied McIntire's motion to dismiss the restraining order, and the station disappeared from the airwaves.

The FCC's Dilemma in the Oregon Case

Finally, on the subject of religious broadcasting, there was the Albany, Oregon, case. A complaint received in April 1974 alleged that Albany station KRKT was giving free time for broadcasts of Sunday services of the church to which the owner of the station belonged but was charging everyone else for religious broadcasts. Since this would be contrary to the FCC's policy against discrimination among religious faiths, the Complaints and Compliance Division asked the station licensee to comment on the complaint.

Yes, said the station owner, he did carry his own church's services free and he charged everyone else for religious time, but there was a reason. While his application for the station was pending before the commission, he had prayed to God that it would be granted, and he had promised in his prayers that if he got the station, he would carry the services of his church free.

I took the case to the commission, pointing out that the station's practices were contrary to FCC policy but noting that any FCC action on the matter might be distorted in the press. I imagined possible newspaper headlines such as "FCC Reprimands Station Owner for Keeping His Promise to God" or "FCC Orders Station to Stop Church Service Broadcasts."

The members of the commission were skillful at spotting a hot potato. After hearing the facts of the case, they instructed the staff to go back and try to devise a solution that would cause no repercussions. (General counsel was urging the commission to drop the whole matter on the grounds that it was de minimis, which is legal jargon for "not important enough to bother about.")

Before the staff could come up with any bright new ideas on how to deal with the case, the station owner unknowingly got the commission off the hook. He wrote that he had had a disagreement with his church and had dropped the broadcasts of its Sunday services.

The FCC breathed a sigh of relief.

7

The FCC and Congress

Commissioner Robert E. Lee was in many ways the most reluctant of regulators but he was all for strict enforcement with respect to a few broadcast practices. One was obscene, indecent, or suggestive program material. Another was rock songs that promoted or condoned the use of drugs. A third was overcommercialism.

In 1963 Lee persuaded the commission to propose rules to establish time limits on broadcast advertising. The proposed standard was the one already adopted by the principal industry trade group, the National Association of Broadcasters. In recognizing the industry's own standards, Lee and his fellow commissioners thought they were on safe ground.

They soon learned better. Stirred up by editorials in *Broadcasting* magazine and by the oratory of some ruggedly individualistic station owners, the broadcasters mounted a massive lobbying campaign on Capitol Hill. Congressman Walter Rogers introduced a bill to prohibit adoption of any limits on commercial time. It passed by the overwhelming vote of 317 to 43, and even before the Senate could consider it, the commissioners saw the handwriting on the wall. They hastily buried their proposal and never dared to disinter it, although the commercials grew longer and longer as the years rolled by.

As a creature of Congress, the FCC has been subservient to it, sometimes to the point of becoming its cat's-paw or whipping boy. It should, of course, also be noted that congressional supervision of the FCC often has served the public interest by holding it up for public scrutiny via the hearing process.

A full account of the commission's relations with the Congress would fill several volumes. For purposes of illustration, a few examples are cited in this chapter.

Dies and Cox Go After the FCC

Early in 1943 the commission and its chairman, James Lawrence Fly, drew the simultaneous ire of two powerful members of the House of Representatives—Martin Dies of Texas, chairman of the Un-American Affairs Committee, and Edward E. Cox of Georgia, a member of the Rules Committee.

According to contemporary newspaper accounts, Dies, a forerunner of Senator Joseph McCarthy in the witch-hunting field, professed to believe that the FCC harbored communists. Cox denounced the agency as "incompetent, arbitrary, inefficient, and a danger and menace to national security." He also accused it of seeking "terroristic control" of all media, an apparent reference to the commission's efforts to limit ownership of radio stations by newspapers and to curtail the power of the networks over their affiliated stations.

Chairman Fly was not one to wilt before congressional demagoguery. He sent investigators to Station WALB, Albany, Georgia, where they found a canceled check from the station to Cox for $2,500 in payment for his assistance in obtaining its license. This was in violation of a federal law prohibiting members of Congress from accepting fees for work before a federal agency.

Fly sent photostats of the check to the Department of Justice and to Sam Rayburn, Speaker of the House. The Justice Department ignored the matter, while Rayburn referred it to the

House Judiciary Committee. This committee declared it had no jurisdiction.

Matters might have rested there had it not been for the *Washington Post.* The *Post* published a front-page editorial titled "A Public Letter to Speaker Rayburn" that said, among other things, "In the opinion of no qualified and dispassionate observer has this investigation been anything but a mockery of basic American traditions of fair play. It has been a star chamber; it has been black with bias; it has sought to terrorize those who exposed [Cox's] corrupt practices."[1]

Four days later Cox resigned, complaining that "poisoned shafts of slander have driven into my heart."[2]

The commission has served as Congress's pawn as well as its scapegoat.

For years, congressional appropriations committees badgered the FCC to charge fees for issuing licenses to those required by law to obtain them. The committees seemed to think that the Federal Communications Commission, alone among all agencies and departments of government, should become self-supporting by levying assessments on those whom it regulated, whether they be youthful amateurs operating ham sets in their attics or giant corporations owning multiple television and radio stations.

The FCC at length yielded to this pressure and adopted rules that set fees for licenses in both the broadcast and non-broadcast fields.[3] The scheme did not long survive. The courts held it to be illegal, and the commission was forced to refund all fees it had collected.[4] Of course, Congress could have adopted a statute to achieve the desired result legally, but it preferred to place the onus on the FCC.

Pastore Gets Rid of a Hot Potato

Senator John Pastore of Rhode Island, chairman of the Communications Subcommittee of the Senate Commerce Committee, once used the commission in this way.

In 1968 the FCC handed down a decision stripping the *Boston Herald-Traveler* of Station WHDH-TV and awarding the license to another applicant.[5] This was a unique case and not a license-renewal challenge, but it caused the television industry to panic over the possibility that TV station owners thereafter might lose their licenses at renewal time to those who filed competing applications. The Communications Act of 1934 permits anyone to file a competing application for a radio or TV license at the end of each license period. Theoretically, if the challenger can prove in a hearing that he or she is likely to serve the public interest better than the incumbent licensee, he or she will be awarded the license. In fact, the commission never has taken away a television license in such a proceeding, but the broadcasters professed to believe that the WHDH decision heralded their destruction. They ran to Congress seeking relief.

Pastore had been principally concerned up to that time about television programs that he considered to be obscene, indecent or, at least, too sexy to meet his moral standards. He hinted to the broadcasters that if they would be more circumspect in their programming, he might help them avoid license confrontations, but he eventually succumbed to their pleas and introduced a bill that would largely have insulated them from license challenges. In substance, the bill provided that a licensee could not be forced to defend itself in a comparative hearing unless the commission first had determined that its record was so bad that its license should be revoked anyway, regardless of the merits of any other applicant. Thus, if a station had met the commission's minimal standards, it would not have to defend itself against the "pie-in-the-sky" promises of a competing applicant.

Pastore received a shock when he held hearings on his bill. Blacks and other ethnic groups charged him with racism, since the bill would tend to prevent minority groups, as well as others, from challenging licenses. Many license challenges at that time were based on the alleged failure of TV stations to employ enough minority staff members or to provide sufficient programming for minority members of their audiences. By filing competing applications, the ethnic groups could, conceivably, win TV licenses. More realistically, they were likely to gain substantial concessions from existing stations in hiring and programming practices. Even though an incumbent might retain his license after a hearing, the legal expenses of this long, drawn-out process might run to well over a million dollars. The wiser course often was to grant concessions to the competing applicants in return for withdrawing their challenges.

Pastore, a colorful politician of Italian ancestry, always had prided himself on being a friend of minorities. He was appalled at the charge of racism now hurled at him. He hit upon a solution, however; hand the hot potato to the Federal Communications Commission.

And thus it was that, after some surreptitious senatorial persuasion, the FCC found itself carrying the ball while Pastore allowed his bill to expire. The commission issued the "Policy Statement Concerning Comparative Hearings Involving Regular Renewal Applications."[6] This was a variation of the Pastore bill in that it would have protected existing licensees against renewal challenges. But it was not destined to fare any better than the FCC's effort to impose licensing fees. The U.S. Court of Appeals struck it down as contrary to the provisions of the Communications Act.[7]

1958–1959 "Oversight" Hearings

Congressional attention to the FCC has often had a most salutary effect on the agency, chiefly through the public hearing process. An example is the series of hearings held in 1958 and 1959 by the Legislative Oversight Committee of the House Committee on Interstate and Foreign Commerce. (The term "oversight" referred to the authority of Congress to oversee the agencies it had created.)

Ironically, some of the most damaging evidence against the FCC in these hearings was revealed over the opposition of most members of the subcommittee and of the chairman of the parent committee, Representative Oren Harris of Arkansas.

Harris and Speaker Sam Rayburn had planned an essentially innocuous inquiry into the operation of the independent agencies. Harris made a mistake, however, in choosing as chief counsel of the subcommittee Bernard Schwartz, a law professor from New York University.

Schwartz proved to be an eager beaver who chose to take the subcommittee's stated objectives literally and proceeded to investigate not only the modus operandi of the agencies but the personal improprieties of their members as well. He began with the FCC, in part because he had read an article in the September 1957 issue of *Harper's* magazine titled "The Scandal in TV Licensing." It had been written by an authority on administrative law, Professor Louis L. Jaffe of the Harvard School of Law.

Schwartz's investigation of the FCC revealed that it often had twisted its policies in order to justify the granting of TV licenses for political reasons. It also revealed that some individual commissioners had broken the law and others had done things that were questionable. For example, some of the sitting commissioners had accepted travel expenses from the broadcast industry that they regulated and later had turned in government expense accounts for the same trips. The U.S. comptroller said this was illegal.

Commissioner John C. Doerfer was one of those guilty of this practice. He had accepted an invitation from TV station KWTV, Oklahoma City, to attend the dedication of its new tower in October 1954. One day later he spoke in Spokane, Washington, at a meeting of the National Association of Radio and Television Broadcasters (now the National Association of Broadcasters). Accompanied by Mrs. Doerfer, he went to Oklahoma City, on to Spokane, and back to Washington.

KWTV paid travel, hotel, and incidental expenses from Washington to Oklahoma City and return. The broadcasters' association paid the Doerfer hotel bill in Spokane plus $575 for other expenses including round-trip airfare for the Doerfers between Washington and Spokane. On his return to Washington Doerfer turned in an expense account to the FCC for the whole trip. Thus, he obtained double reimbursement; in fact, he received money from all three sources for part of the Spokane-to-Washington leg of the junket.

Doerfer seemed to see nothing wrong with this. He admitted he had received outside payments for at least a dozen trips for which he also had collected travel expenses from the government.[8] Nevertheless, he had been elevated in 1957 to the chairmanship of the commission.

Eventually, President Dwight Eisenhower asked for his resignation after the hearings also brought to light the fact that Doerfer and his wife had spent a vacation on the Florida yacht of George B. Storer, owner of several TV and radio stations. At the time Storer had a case pending before the FCC.

Schwartz's efforts to learn what other favors the FCC commissioners had accepted were hampered by the fact that they alone among members of the six agencies being investigated refused to answer the financial questionnaires the subcommittee sent them. Schwartz then tried to obtain the answers by subpoena but Commerce Committee Chairman Oren Harris refused to sign the subpoenas. Despite this and other roadblocks, Schwartz was able, in the period between his appointment as subcommittee counsel and his dismissal for being too zealous, to uncover many examples of improper conduct by commissioners.

He revealed that FCC chairman George C. McConnaughey had asked CBS, a licensee of the commission, to give a job to his son, who had no broadcast experience. He finally obtained a job for the son at a Michigan station that had a case pending before the commission.[9]

He also disclosed that members of the commission received free color television sets from RCA and its subsidiary, NBC.[10] An ironical sidelight on this was revealed to the author years later. At the height of the hubbub over the acceptance by commissioners of the RCA sets, Chairman Harris of the Commerce Committee had an aide quietly request the Westinghouse Electric Corporation to send someone out to Harris's home to take back the color TV set that Westinghouse had furnished to him.[11]

Oren Harris Buys Some TV Stock

Harris had become involved in a much more gross act of venality. Shortly after becoming chairman of the Commerce Committee, he had bought a 25 percent interest in Station KRBB-TV, El Dorado, Arkansas, for the remarkably low price of $500 in cash and a promissory note for $4,500. Before Harris acquired this interest, the station's application for an increase in power had been turned down by the FCC on the grounds that KRBB was not "financially qualified." After Harris got his cut, the station filed another application. This one was approved. Somehow its financial condition had miraculously improved as soon as Harris became part owner. The station received a $400,000 line of credit from a bank, and RCA, which manufactured TV transmitters, decided to advance it another line of credit for $200,000.

Schwartz states in his book *The Professor and the Commissions* that it was he who told newspaper reporters about the Harris TV deal.[12] The result was that an embarrassed Harris announced he was selling his interest for what he had paid for it. He complained of "harassment" by the press.

The most flagrant example of misconduct by a member of the FCC was that of Richard A. Mack who, like Doerfer and McConnaughey, was an Eisenhower appointee. Mack had accepted bribes from Miami attorney Thurman A. Whiteside, who had been retained by National Airlines to help it get a Miami TV license that was being sought by four applicants.

Altogether, Mack received cash and stock worth about twenty thousand dollars from Whiteside during pendency of this case in return for his promise to vote to award the Channel 10 license to National Airlines. Learning of this arrangement, one of the opposing applicants sent two friends of Mack to Washington to try to persuade him to "seek a release" from his "pledge" to Whiteside. The pliant Mack asked Whiteside to release him, but Whiteside refused and Mack dutifully voted for National Airlines.[13]

The Miami Channel 10 case was typical of those described

in Chapter 2 in which the commission weighted its criteria for applicants in contested TV cases so as to reach a predetermined conclusion. National Airlines probably was the least eligible of the four applicants under the commission's published standards. The hearing examiner ruled in favor of another applicant but, as often happened in such cases in that era, the commission overruled him.

According to Schwartz, this was one of seventeen questionable FCC licensing decisions that he had investigated and on which he proposed to hold public hearings. But it was the only one made public before Harris and the majority of the subcommittee fired him.

The way in which Harris went about getting him fired and Schwartz's efforts to place the results of his investigation before the public make an intriguing story.

On the basis of his investigation to that date, Schwartz dictated a twenty-eight–page memorandum to the subcommittee on January 4, 1958, summarizing his findings and outlining the subjects he proposed to go into during public hearings. But when he went to the next meeting, he ran into a hornet's nest. Most committee members were aghast at the idea of exposing improprieties by individual commissioners. Only Morgan Moulder, chairman of the subcommittee, and Congressmen John Moss and Peter Mack supported Schwartz. Harris said he wanted a "broad, general survey" of the agencies, which would avoid inquiry into possible misconduct by individual commissioners. The majority voted to limit the hearings to this concept.

Public Hearings Begin

Thus matters stood until columnist Drew Pearson published extracts from Schwartz's memo to the committee. Schwartz said he did not give the memo to any member of the press until Pearson had printed parts of it, but that at that point he supplied the full memo to the *New York Times* in return for a promise to give it front-page treatment and to publish the full text. Publication of the memo by the *Times* forced Harris to change his position and announce that public hearings on possible misconduct at the FCC would begin the following week.

Chairman Doerfer was the first witness. During testimony given February 3, 4, and 5, 1958, Schwartz forced him to admit receiving double reimbursement for travel expenses, as well as the vacation aboard Storer's yacht. Schwartz next planned to go into the bribery of Commissioner Mack in the Miami case, but the subcommittee fired him on the grounds that he had violated House rules by releasing his memorandum to the *New York Times*. Subcommittee Chairman Morgan Moulder resigned from his post in protest.[14]

Schwartz now began to fear that the subcommittee would seize and suppress the records of his investigation. He learned that it was about to subpoena him to appear before it with his files. At this point Clark Mollenhoff, then Washington correspondent of the *Des Moines Register,* telephoned to say that Senator John T. Williams of Delaware wanted to see the files. Schwartz writes,

Thus began the now celebrated odyssey of the Subcommittee files. Mollenhoff and I carted the documents, packed in a large overseas case and two cardboard boxes, to Senator Williams' apartment at about 9:30 p.m. The investigation-minded Republican Senator looked over the files and listened to my explanation of what was in them. At this point there was a phone call from my wife, transmitting a request from Senator Morse of Oregon that I bring the files to him. This request had been forwarded through Jack Anderson, Drew Pearson's principal associate.

Off Mollenhoff and I went to Senator Morse's apartment, picking up Anderson on the way. We arrived there after eleven p.m. Morse, after finding out what I had brought, asked me to leave the materials with him. I readily concurred.

What were my aims in handing my files over to Senator Morse? In view of my opinion as to the main motives of the Subcommittee, I felt it essential that the files not be turned back to their unfettered discretion. If copies of my main materials could be seen by a member of the Senate, it would make suppression of it on the House side much more difficult. . . . I could make sure that the Subcommittee would at least think twice before going ahead baldly with their plans to squelch the investigation.[15]

When Schwartz got home after midnight, a U.S. marshall handed him a subpoena calling for his appearance before the subcommittee the next morning with all files and records. He appeared but without the records. When asked where they were, he replied that Senator Morse had them. He writes in his book, "It was so quiet at this point that you could have heard a Congressman drop. And several of them, in their distress, looked as though they might do just that."[16]

After he left the session that afternoon, Schwartz told reporters that the subcommittee had fired him in order to squelch the investigation, "knowing that I have secured evidence of the payment of money to a Federal Communications Commissioner in a television case."

Publication of this charge forced the subcommittee to call him before it in a crowded public hearing two days later and, in effect, to order him to put up or shut up. In the absence of his files, Schwartz had to rely on his memory in bringing out the details of Mack's acceptance of bribes, but he was so familiar with them that he was able to tick off the essential facts.

By this time, the cumulative revelations of official misconduct and the subcommittee's efforts to suppress them had placed Harris and the committee in an untenable position. Speaker Rayburn decided that the integrity of the House of Representatives itself was now in question, and he directed Harris to hold public hearings on the matters Schwartz had unearthed, but with new subcommittee counsel.

Rigged Quiz Programs

The hearings later shifted from the subject of FCC misdeeds to rigged TV quiz programs and payola. Drew Pearson charged in his column that Harris got into the sensational revelations of payola and fake quiz programs in order to divert the public's attention from the subcommittee's attempt to suppress the Schwartz investigation. Whatever the motivation, the hearings revealed that the scholarly young Charles Van Doren, hero of NBC's program "Twenty-One," had been given the answers to the questions before each broadcast and even had been coached on how to fake the appearance of uncertainty and nervousness as he ostensibly racked his brain for the correct answers.

The "$64,000 Question" on CBS likewise was exposed as a fraud.

During the rigged quiz hearings, a chance remark by one witness led the committee into another line of inquiry that revealed what a good many people in the broadcasting and music businesses already knew: some of the best-known disc jockeys in the country were accepting bribes for playing records. The committee found that during 1958 and 1959 some 1,300 record distributors had paid $263,244 in payola to get their records plugged in twenty-three cities.

One result of the quiz show and payola revelations was the enactment of two new sections of the Communications Act. One required that acceptance of all payments for the broadcast of any matter (i.e., payola) be disclosed on the air at the time of the broadcast.[17] The other forbade prearranging the outcome of any contest of chance or "intellectual skill."[18] Significantly omitted from the scope of this statute were fraudulent athletic contests. Perhaps this was because most TV stations at the time were broadcasting professional wrestling matches, which almost everybody knew were faked; but Congress didn't want to get into the matter.

Both new sections provided fines and/or imprisonment for individuals violating them, and Section 312(a) already authorized the commission to revoke station licenses for willful or repeated violation of any part of the act.

The subcommittee hearings embarrassed the FCC in many ways. First, there were the revelations of the bribery of Mack, the acceptance by other commissioners of favors from broadcasters, and political favoritism in granting licenses. Then came the quiz show and payola scandals, which revealed that the commission either had not known or had not cared about widespread deception of the public by its licensees.

In an effort to avert future embarrassment, the FCC established a new division in 1960 that bore the awkward title of Complaints and Compliance Division. Its purpose was to bring about better enforcement of the law by investigating complaints against broadcasters and recommending to the commission what to do about them. Almost all of the violations cited in this volume that took place after 1960 were unearthed by this division of the Broadcast Bureau.

The congressional committees with responsibility for overseeing the activities of the commission have held additional hearings in recent years on some of its unprecedented actions. During the latter part of President Reagan's second term, relations between Congress and the commission became so strained that the president dared not submit his last two appointments of commissioners to the Senate for confirmation, thus leaving the commission with only three members.

8

The Reagan Commission: A National Disgrace

Soon after President Ronald Reagan appointed Mark Fowler as chairman of the Federal Communications Commission in 1981, veteran observers of the agency began to have a sense of deja vu. The wheel had come full turn and they were witnessing the advent of another do-nothing commission as they had during the Eisenhower administration. In a sense, they were wrong. The Reagan commission was not idle. It was busily reinterpreting the Communications Act so as to dismantle much of the structure of broadcast regulation.

After two decades of superior chairmen—most notably, Newton N. Minow and Richard E. Wiley—the commission already had started downhill during the Carter administration. With Reagan's appointment of Fowler and Dennis Patrick as successive chairmen, it became a national disgrace.

Preceding chapters have told how the commission refused to enforce the fairness doctrine and eventually declared it "unconstitutional," how for years it misinterpreted a landmark Supreme Court decision on the broadcast of indecent language and summarily rejected all complaints on that subject, and how it refused to expose the fraudulent practices of TV evangelist Jim

Bakker and let him continue to misappropriate contributions of his followers until he was detected in a different type of offense.

The commission has acted in more fundamental ways than these to undermine the basic principles of broadcast regulation as set forth in the Communications Act of 1934 and affirmed by the Supreme Court. It has sought to nullify the entire concept that a broadcaster is a public trustee and must serve the public interest in return for being allowed to use one of the limited number of frequencies in the radio spectrum.

Here are examples of what the commission has done — and not done — in its slide toward regulatory oblivion.

Character Qualifications

If a broadcaster is to act as a trustee for the community, one might reasonably expect him or her to possess character qualifications that would enable him or her to fill that role; at the least, that the broadcaster's record contain no evidence of fraudulent conduct, material misrepresentations on matters of importance, discriminatory practices, or other failings that might raise doubts on fitness to hold a license. The Communications Act says that all applications for station licenses "shall set forth such facts as the Commission . . . may prescribe as to the citizenship, character, and financial, technical and other qualifications of the applicant to operate the station."[1]

The commission had interpreted the word "character" to mean what the dictionary says it does: "good moral constitution or status," "reputation," "good repute."[2] In December 1985, however, the commission announced that in the future "the scope of our analysis [of character qualifications] will be much narrower than the term 'character' implies."[3] The only facts it would consider as possibly disqualifying an applicant were *adjudicated* findings of felony, misconduct of a "broadcast related nature," or misrepresentations to the commission itself. Misdemeanors would be disregarded, as would felonies, unless the applicant had been finally and irrevocably convicted. If a defendant had signed a consent decree under which prosecution was dropped in return for his promise not to commit the alleged violation in the future, the FCC would ignore the case. If the statute of limitations prevented prosecution for an alleged felony, that case would not count, either, nor would a felony charge reduced to a misdemeanor because of plea bargaining. A judgment against an applicant for fraud in a civil case would be disregarded, no matter how badly it reflected on his or her character. As a Washington communications attorney told me, "You can bring in a videotape of somebody taking a bribe, but it won't count with the FCC unless he has been convicted in court."

Trafficking in Licenses

The commission long held that since broadcast licenses are granted to serve the public interest, persons applying for them should intend to do just that—to operate their stations rather than to make a fast buck by a quick sale to someone else. In 1962 the commission adopted an "antitrafficking" rule that effectively prevented sales of stations within less than three years of their acquisition, unless special circumstances existed such as financial hardship.[4]

Twenty years later the Reagan commission abolished the rule,[5] with the results that might have been expected. Wall Street speculators began buying stations, eliminating most live and public affairs programs, firing the staff members who had produced such programs, and then, having cut costs and improved the bottom line, quickly selling the stations for a profit.

Representative Al Swift of Washington introduced a bill to compel the commission to reinstate the antitrafficking rule. Hearings on it were held in June 1987 before the House Subcommittee on Telecommunications and Finance.[6] Chairman Edward J. Markey of the subcommittee cited statistics revealing that within four years of the abolition of the rule the number of television stations sold annually after being held less than two years had increased almost eightfold. Said Markey,

These statistics . . . represent only a small glimpse of the trading frenzy that has plagued the broadcast industry over the past several years. . . . Broadcast licenses are different from pork bellies or soybean futures. A license to use the public airwaves is a privilege. . . . Broadcast licensees cannot possibly meet their public interest obligations if they are constantly transferring their licenses. . . . Short-term, fast-buck artists do not have the time, the inclination or economic incentive to meet the needs of the communities they serve.

Hostile Takeovers of Stations

The commission has found still other ways to make possible the speculation in broadcast licenses. One is by permitting the mania for hostile takeovers of corporations to spread to the broadcast field. In the Storer case,[7] it allowed a group of financiers who held only 5.3 percent of the stock of the licensee corporation to obtain control of it in a takeover maneuver that evaded normal statutory requirements for seeking transfer of control of a licensee. To accomplish this the commission thought up a new interpretation to Section 309 of the Communications Act.

The group that thus obtained control of the corporation had made no secret of its intention to sell off the seven Storer TV stations as quickly as possible for a profit. So much for the commission's traditional stand against trafficking in licenses. The decision also seemed to mean that thereafter no publicly held licensee corporation could be secure against Wall Street raiders.

In 1986 the commission issued the "Policy Statement on Tender Offers and Proxy Contests" extending its rationale in Storer to other takeover cases.[8] An appeal was filed by the Office of Communication of the United Church of Christ and two other groups, challenging the legal basis for the policy statement and charging that "in practice, the commission is simply furthering private business interests without regard to the public interest."

The appellants and the commission itself both urged the court to rule on the appeal so as to settle the question once and for all. But Judge Robert Bork found that the issues raised were not "ripe" for judicial consideration because the commission had not yet applied its policy statement in a particular proceeding.[9]

CBS and Laurence Tisch

In the Storer case the FCC allowed raiders who held only 5.3 percent of the voting stock to obtain control of the corporation, although they proposed to replace the existing board of directors. The commission said that control of the corporation lay with the stockholders, and since the raiding group was only seeking the proxies of the stockholders in order to elect a new board, there was no transfer of control.

Along came two other cases in which the commission took exactly the opposite position, saying that control of the large corporations in these cases resided in the board of directors and *not* the stockholders. One was the Metromedia case,[10] the other involved acquisition of 24.9 percent of the stock of the Columbia Broadcasting System by Laurence Tisch, billionaire corporation trader. The commission ruled that acquisition of the stock by Tisch did not give him control of the network and therefore no application need have been filed for transfer of control.

An organization called Fairness in Media (FIM) claimed that Tisch had obtained de facto control because 25 percent ownership of a huge, widely held corporation generally is sufficient to gain control and that, in fact, Tisch had been in charge at CBS for some time, having brought about the removal of the former board chairman and made himself chief executive officer.

The FCC held that no transfer of control had taken place.[11] One well-known Washington communications attorney commented, "Everybody on Wall Street and everybody in Washington except the FCC knows that if you own 25 percent of the stock of a large, publicly-held corporation you have control of it." Peter J. Boyer in his book *Who Killed CBS?* lists these changes that took place at CBS after Tisch moved in:[12]

1. It sold off its publishing operations and its highly successful CBS Records Division

2. It pulled out of Trintex, its joint venture with IBM and Sears to develop a nationwide videotex system

3. It fired 215 employees of CBS news in March 1987 and cut the news budget almost thirty-three million dollars (the third major news cutback in sixteen months)

Most broadcasters traditionally have had an ambivalent attitude toward the business of operating radio stations. On the one hand, they gloried in the praise they got for public service including awards for their news and public affairs programs. On the other hand, they were in business to make money, and most of them made a good deal of money in light of their original investments while still trying to fulfill their obligation to the public interest. Then the bottom-line boys moved in and public interest went out the window.

A nationwide survey by the Radio-Television News Directors' Association revealed a significant drop in public affairs programming after the commission "deregulated" the medium. Its study found that in 1985, 30 percent of all independent (non-network-affiliated) television stations had no news staffs. One year later the figure had risen to 37 percent. Some two thousand full-time staff members had lost their jobs in radio newsrooms—replaced by seven hundred part-time employees.[13]

In view of the commission's recent reversal of traditional policies it is not surprising that stations have been changing hands rapidly at escalating prices. The New York investment banking firm of Kohlberg, Kravis, Roberts & Co. (KKR) is one of the best-known specialists in "in-and-out" station trading. It sold KTLA-TV, Los Angeles, in December 1985 for $529 million in a quick turnover that produced a profit of $250 million. In July 1984 SNF Companies paid $125 million for WFTV-TV, Orlando, Florida. Fourteen months later SNF sold it for $185 million.

Or consider the case of KITN-TV, Minneapolis. The original owners operated it for only eighteen months at a total outlay of $175,000 in cash and $3 million in bank loans. They sold it in February 1984 for $12 million to Beverly Hills Hotel Corporation, which was controlled by Wall Street arbitrager Ivan Boesky (who later went to prison on insider trading charges). Beverly Hills resold the station in 1985 for $24 million.

In 1984 KKR bought KVOS-TV, Bellingham, Washington, which it kept for approximately one year before selling it. Meanwhile, it had cut the station's staff from ninety to sixty-five persons and replaced its thirty-minute daily newscast with sixty-second "newsbreaks."[14]

Children's Programs

Previous commissions had given special attention to children's programming. In a 1971 proceeding the commission said that such programming should reflect "the high public interest considerations involved in the use of television, perhaps the most powerful communications medium ever devised, in relation to a large and important segment of the audience, the nation's children."[15]

Three years later the FCC issued guidelines on the amount of advertising to be broadcast on such programs and warned against presenting advertising disguised as program material. It also directed broadcasters to schedule some informational children's programs in addition to those intended solely to entertain.[16]

Along came the Reagan administration, and the requirements for informational programming, as well as the guidelines on maximum commercial content, were dropped.[17]

In dissenting to the commission's order abandoning regulation of children's programming, Commissioner Henry M. Rivera wrote, "I wish I had the eloquence of a Mark Antony for this eulogy. Our federal children's television policy commitment deserves no less at this, its interment. Make no mistake—this is a funeral and my colleagues have here written the epitaph of the FCC's involvement in children's programming."

An organization called Action for Children's Television appealed the commission's decision, and the D.C. Circuit Court of Appeals remanded the case to the commission, where it now sits. The court said, "We find that the commission has failed to explain adequately the elimination of its long-standing children's television commercialization guidelines."[18]

On June 8, 1988, the House approved, 328 to 78, a bill to reimpose limits on advertising during children's programs. The bill would have limited commercials to twelve minutes per hour on weekdays and twelve and one-half minutes on weekends. It also would have required the FCC to consider, in license renewal procedures, whether a station had served the educational needs of children in its overall programming. The Senate passed the bill by a voice vote in October but on November 5, 1988, President Reagan exercised a pocket veto of the legislation.[19]

"Let the Marketplace Decide"

The commission has cited various grounds for throwing broadcast regulation overboard. In abandoning a number of rules and policies that it termed "regulatory underbrush," the FCC said it lacked the resources and expertise to deal with matters like false advertising or fraudulent billing of advertisers by licensees. It said some of these rules represented "an unnecessary and unwarranted intrusion into the business operations of licensees" and others "may have unwittingly obstructed economic efficiencies." Let the Federal Trade Commission (FTC), the Department of Justice, or some other arm of government handle such problems, if they existed.[20]

Yet predecessor commissions had managed to give attention to these subjects. As for passing the buck to other agencies, the commissioners must be aware that under President Reagan the FTC and the Justice Department were as disinclined to enforce laws against business interests as the FCC and could hardly be expected to assume additional responsibilities.

The justification recited most often for abandoning regulation is that competition in the marketplace will correct whatever deficiencies may exist. This marketplace rationale did not originate with Mark Fowler or Dennis Patrick. It was first advanced by Chairman Charles Ferris under the Carter administration, but Fowler and Patrick eagerly embraced it.

It is, of course, true that competition in the market controls most elements of a capitalist economy, for example, what products, and how many, will be offered. However, the commission's reliance on marketplace forces disregards the fact that the laws enacted by Congress to regulate some aspects of broadcasting and other business activities are based on precisely the opposite assumption: that in some areas government regulation is required in order to protect the public. If the FCC's current rationale were carried to its logical conclusion, the Federal Aviation Administration should stop requiring maintenance and inspection of passenger planes. If Airline XXX has too many fatal crashes, the free play of the market will correct the situation because people will stop riding on the planes of that airline. The whole purpose of the Communications Act of 1934 was to make sure that the "free forces of the marketplace" did not entirely control radio because broadcasting is affected by the public interest.

The extent to which the commission has nullified broadcast regulation has received little attention in the daily press. It has received more in Congress, where hearings have been held on some of its actions and legislation passed in such matters as restoring the fairness doctrine and limiting commercials on children's programs.

The courts have been more active. According to a study made by the Congressional Research Service (CRS) in January

1988, the U.S. Circuit Court of Appeals for the D.C. circuit had, since January 1986, either reversed or remanded to the commission twenty-two of the approximately eighty FCC decisions that reached that court, surely a record for a period of two years.[21]

In releasing the CRS report, Chairman Edward J. Markey of the House Subcommittee on Telecommunications and Finance said,

> The Congress has long stated its opposition to the Reagan FCC's seemingly rabid pursuit of policy solely on the basis of ideology instead of reason and fact. Now this CRS report reveals the U.S. judiciary has joined in this criticism. It is time for the FCC to take seriously its statutory duties once and for all and to abandon its current strategy of bypassing all that is essential to informed and publicly-minded regulatory policy.[22]

One final note: as explained at the end of Chapter 7, following the House Oversight Committee hearings in 1958 and 1959, the commission created a new division to process complaints, investigate alleged violations by broadcasters, and report them to the commission with recommendations for sanctions if they seemed to merit such action. Shortly after Fowler arrived, the division was merged with another one and its investigative function was effectively eliminated.

Many allegations against broadcasters can be confirmed or proved false only by means of on-the-site field investigations. Under the Reagan administration such investigations ceased almost entirely. If a serious violation was alleged against a licensee, the procedure became one of merely sending a letter reciting the allegation and asking his or her comments on it. Since the licensee knew that the commission would make no field investigation, there was strong motivation simply to mail back a denial of the violation. This would terminate the commission's inquiry.

Thus, an agency with an unparalleled record of ups and downs in the exercise of its regulatory responsibilities reached perhaps the lowest point of its history during the Reagan administration. Observers will watch closely to see what it does during the Bush administration.

Notes

Since the bibliography gives full citations, the notes on the following pages are made as brief as clarity permits. Books are cited by the names of authors. The most frequently cited legal sources are listed by their customary abbreviations, as follows:

C.F.R.	Code of Federal Regulations
Cong. Rec.	Congressional Record
F., F.2d	Federal Reporter, first and second series (Circuit Courts of Appeal)
FCC, FCC 2d	Federal Communications Commission Reports, first and second series
FCC Rcd.	Reports of FCC cases since Oct. 1, 1986
Fed. Reg.	Federal Register
FRC	Federal Radio Commission Reports
RR, RR 2d	Pike & Fischer *Radio Regulation* (FCC actions)
S. Ct.	Supreme Court Reports (Supreme Court)
Serg. & R.	Sergeant & Rawl (Pennsylvania court reporters from 1814 to 1828)
Stat.	U. S. Statutes
U.S.	United States Reports (Supreme Court)
U.S.C.	United States Code
U.S.L.W.	U.S. Law Week (Supreme Court)

Introduction

1. Minow, 8.
2. Communications Act of 1934, as amended (47 U.S.C.); Administrative Procedure Act (5 U.S.C. 551–59); 47 C.F.R.

Chapter 1

1. CBS ("Hunger in America"), 20 FCC 2d 143 (1969).
2. Id., 145.
3. CBS ("Selling of the Pentagon"), 30 FCC 2d 150 (1971).
4. Mayer, 259.
5. 47 U.S.C. 309(a).
6. CBS ("Hunger"), *supra,* 151.
7. Id., 151.
8. Letter to Cong. Staggers, 30 FCC 2d, 150, 153 (1971).
9. CBS ("Hunger"), *supra,* 151.
10. 32 FCC 706, 707–8 (1962).
11. 34 FCC 1039; *aff'd.,* 337 F.2d 540 (1964); *cert. den.,* 380 U.S. 343 (1964).
12. 15 FCC 2d 120 (1968); *recon. den.,* 17 FCC 2d 485; *aff'd., sub nom. Continental Broadcasting Co.* v. *FCC,* 439 F.2d 580; *cert. den.,* 403 U.S. 905 (1971).
13. Id., 131.
14. CBS ("Hunger"), *supra,* 147, 151.
15. CBS ("Selling"), *supra,* 152.
16. Id., 153.
17. Mayer, 269.
18. Cong. Rec., H6953, July 12, 1971.
19. 4 RR 1313; 5 RR 1292; 6 RR 38(b), 129, 415, 1105, 1286; 7 RR 313, 788.
20. Testimony of ex-employees of KMPC in Docket No. 9468, File No. BR-18, KMPC, Station of the Stars, Inc., FCC docket files.
21. Barnouw, II, 119.
22. CBS (WBBM-TV "Pot Party"), 18 FCC 2d 124 (1969).
23. Letter to ABC, CBS, NBC, 16 FCC 2d 650 (1969).
24. CBS Tennis, 69 FCC 2d 1082, 1091 (1978).
25. Id., 1092.
26. Id., 1093.
27. Letter to ABC, 42 RR 2d 1433 (1978).
28. Citizens' Firearms Council, 29 FCC 2d 242 (1971).
29. KRON-TV, 40 FCC 2d 775 (1973).
30. WPIX-TV, 68 FCC 2d 218, 381 (1978).
31. Id., 419–25.
32. WJIM-TV, 92 FCC 2d 248 (1981).
33. Id., 204.
34. Efron, *News Twisters* 108.
35. Id., 106.

Chapter 2

1. Minow, 36.
2. Barnouw, II, 170.
3. Star-Times Pub. Co., 3 FCC 349 (1936).
4. Told to the author by Ray V. Hamilton, whose life-long career in broadcasting included network staff positions and ownership of a major TV and radio station brokerage firm.
5. The source of much of the information herein on KWKH and Henderson is C. Joseph Pusateri's *Enterprise in Radio: WWL and the Business of Broadcasting in America.*
6. Told to the author by George S. Smith, former Chief of the Broadcast Bureau of the FCC and, earlier in his career, junior partner in Segal & Smith, counsel for WWL.
7. Broadcasting Publications, Inc., ix.
8. Dugger, 268.
9. *Broadcasting Yearbook,* 1944, 1946.
10. *Sixth Report and Order,* 41 FCC 148 (1952).
11. *Broadcasting-Telecasting Yearbook,* 1953–54.
12. Report and Order, 41 FCC 893 (1960).
13. *Telecasting Yearbook,* 1955–56, 357.
14. Report and Order, 41 FCC 787.
15. *Broadcasting-Telecasting Yearbook,* 1952–53.
16. Told to the author by William H. Hunter, former FCC branch chief.
17. KTLA-TV, Los Angeles.
18. Quinlan, 4.
19. Schwartz, 149–56.
20. Id., 191.
21. Id., 77.
22. *Sixth Report and Order, supra,* pars. 739–40.
23. 10 RR 567 (1954); *recon. den.,* 10 RR 584 (1954).
24. *Great Lakes Broadcasting Co.,* 3 FRC 32 (1929); rev. on other grounds, 37 F.2d 993; *cert. dismissed* 281 U.S. 706 (1930).
25. 30 FCC 109 (1961).
26. Schwartz, 156.
27. Id., 157.
28. Id., 157.
29. Quinlan's *The Hundred-Million Dollar Lunch* is devoted entirely to this case.
30. Broadcasting Publications, Inc., *supra,* 196.
31. 3 RR 2d 748 (1963).
32. 3 RR 2d 745 (1964).
33. Star Stations of Indiana, Inc., 19 FCC 2d 991 (1969); 17 RR 2d 491.
34. Star Stations of Indiana, Inc., 51 FCC 2d 95, 108 (1975); 32 RR 2d 1151.

35. Id., 109.
36. File No. 61–3, FRC Division of Mail and Files.
37. Equity Suit No. 51872, S. Ct. of D.C. (1930).
38. *FRC Annual Report,* 1931.
39. Hearing Transcript, 429–30, *Nelson Brothers Bond & Mortgage Co.* v. *FRC,* Ct. of App. of D.C., Oct. term, 1931, nos. 5530, 5533.
40. Id., 129.
41. *Broadcasting,* Dec. 1, 1932; *FRC Annual Report,* 1933, 9.
42. Id., Dec. 1, 1931, 6.
43. Id., Sept. 1, 1932, 13.
44. 62 F.2d 854 (1932); 289 U.S. 266 (1933).

Chapter 3

1. *Commonwealth* v. *Sharpless,* 2 Serg. & R. 91 (1815) (Pennsylvania).
2. 237 F.2d 796; *aff'd.,* 354 U.S. 476 (1957).
3. Id., 489.
4. 383 U.S. 413 (1966).
5. Id., 418.
6. 413 U.S. 15 (1973).
7. Id., 24.
8. Sec. 29, 44 U.S. Stat. 1162.
9. 18 U.S.C. 1464.
10. 47 U.S.C. 312(a) (6).
11. *William B. Schaeffer, d/b/a Schaeffer Radio Co.* v. *FRC,* Case No. 5228 (1930).
12. *Duncan* v. *U.S.,* 48 F.2d 128 (1931); *cert. den.,* 282 U.S. 863, (1931).
13. *Joseph Bursteyn, Inc.* v. *Wilson,* 343 U.S. 495, 505 (1952).
14. *Order to Show Cause,* FCC 59-1224 (1959).
15. Mile High Stations, Inc., 28 FCC 795, 797 (1960).
16. Palmetto Broadcasting Co. (WDKD), 33 FCC 250 (1962); *recon. den.,* 34 FCC 101 (1963); *aff'd. sub nom. E. G. Robinson* v. *FCC,* 334 F.2d 534; *cert. den.,* 379 U.S. 843 (1964).
17. Eastern Education Radio, 24 FCC 2d 408 (1970).
18. Id., 410.
19. Id., 410.
20. Id., 412.
21. Sonderling Broadcasting Corporation, 27 RR 2d 285 (1973); *recon. den.,* 41 FCC 2d 777 (1973).
22. Id., 285.
23. Id., 290.
24. Id., 291.

25. *Illinois Citizens' Committee for Broadcasting* v. *FCC,* 515 F.2d 397 (1975).
26. Trustees of the University of Pennsylvania, 57 FCC 2d 782 (1975).
27. Id., 793.
28. Trustees of the University of Pennsylvania, 71 FCC 2d 416 (1979).
29. *FCC* v. *Pacifica Foundation,* 438 U.S. 726 (1978).
30. 56 FCC 2d 94, 98 (1975).
31. 556 F.2d 9 (1976).
32. 438 U.S. 726 (1978).
33. Id., 747–50.
34. FCC Press Release No. 2823, April 16, 1987. Memorandum Opinions and Orders in these three cases were released April 29, 1987. In the Matter of Pacifica Foundation, Inc. (KFPK-FM), 2 FCC Rcd. 2698 (1987); In the Matter of Infinity Broadcasting Corp. (WYSP-FM), 2 FCC Rcd. 2705 (1987); In the Matter of The Regents of the University of California (KCSB-FM), 2 FCC Rcd. 2703 (1987); *recon. den.,* 3 FCC Rcd. 930 (1987).
35. VIDEO 44, 102 FCC 2d 408 (1985).
36. VIDEO 44, 103 FCC 2d 1204 (1986).
37. VIDEO 44, 3 FCC Rcd., 757 (1988).

Chapter 4

━━━━━━━━━

1. Although fairness doctrine violations were among the charges against the Carl McIntire station, WXUR, two of the three members of the circuit court of appeals panel that upheld the FCC decision to deny renewal of license based their decision on other violations by the licensee (see Chapter 6).
2. For an extensive discussion of the fairness doctrine, see the FCC's 1974 *Fairness Report,* 48 FCC 2d 1 (1974); *recon. den.,* 58 FCC 2d 691 (1976); *aff'd. sub nom. National Citizens Committee for Broadcasting* v. *FCC,* 567 F.2d 1095 (1977); *cert. den.,* 436 U.S. 928 (1978).
3. *Great Lakes Broadcasting Co.,* 3 FRC 32 (1929); reversed on other grounds, 37 F.2d 993; *cert. den.,* 281 U.S. 706 (1930).
4. 13 FCC 1246, 1251 (1949).
5. 47 U.S.C. 315(a).
6. Petition of Sam Morris, 3 RR 154, 155 (1946).
7. Petition of Robert Harold Scott, 11 FCC 372 (1946).
8. Id., 374.
9. Id., 373.
10. Cullman Broadcasting Co., 40 FCC 576 (1963).
11. *Red Lion Broadcasting Co.* v. *FCC,* 395 U.S. 367 (1969).
12. Id., 371, n. 2.
13. 47 C.F.R. 73.123.

14. 47 U.S.C. 315(a).
15. 8 FCC 2d 721 (1967).
16. 12 FCC 2d 250, 252 (1968).
17. WCBS-TV, 8 FCC 2d 381 (1966); *recon. den.*, 9 FCC 2d 921 (1967).
18. *Banzhaf et al.* v. *FCC*, 405 F.2d 1082, 1099 (1968); *cert. den.*, *ABC* v. *FCC*, 396 U.S. 642 (1969).
19. Alan F. Neckritz, 29 FCC 2d 807, 812 (1971); *recon. den.*, 37 FCC 2d, 528 (1972).
20. Friends of the Earth, 24 FCC 2d 743 (1970).
21. *Friends of the Earth* v. *FCC*, 449 F.2d 1164, 1170 (1971).
22. Id., 1170.
23. See Note 2 to this chapter.
24. 48 FCC 2d, 24–26.
25. Committee for Fair Broadcasting of Controversial Issues, 25 FCC 2d 283, 297–98 (1970); *aff'd.* on recon., *sub nom.* Republican National Committee, 25 FCC 2d 739 (1970).
26. Commissioners Robert Bartley and H. Rex Lee were not involved in the deal. They dissented.
27. Republican National Committee, 25 FCC 2d 283 (1970); rev. *sub nom. CBS* v. *FCC*, 454 F.2d, 1018 (1971).
28. In his first eighteen months in office Richard Nixon appeared on prime-time television fourteen times, compared to seven times for Lyndon Johnson in the same length of time, four for John F. Kennedy, and three for Dwight D. Eisenhower.
29. Republican National Committee, *supra,* 300.
30. 454 F.2d 1034–35 (1971).
31. Id., 1035.
32. Id., 1033, n. 87.
33. *RTNDA Communicator,* Oct. 1983, 28.
34. FCC News Release No. 5068, Sept. 17, 1981.
35. *Notice of Inquiry,* 49 Fed. Reg. 20317 (May 14, 1984).
36. *General Fairness Doctrine Obligations of Broadcast Licensees,* 102 FCC 2d 143 (1985).
37. Id., 246–47.
38. *Red Lion, supra,* 381.
39. *CBS* v. *Democratic National Committee,* 412 U.S. 94, 113, n. 12 (1973).
40. President Reagan later nominated Bork for a seat on the Supreme Court, but the Senate rejected him in October 1987 by a vote of 58 to 42.
41. *Telecommunications and Research Action Center* v. *FCC,* 801 F.2d 501 (1986); Rehearing den. 806 F.2d 1115; *cert. den.,* 55 U.S.L.W. 3821 (U.S. 1987).
42. "TRAC," *reh. den.* 806 F.2d 1115.
43. *CBS* v. *Democratic National Committee, supra,* at 129–30.
44. "TRAC," *reh. den., supra,* 1118.
45. *Fairness in Broadcasting Act of 1987:* Report of the Senate Committee on Commerce, Science, and Transportation on S. 742. Report 100-34, 100th Cong., 1st sess., 3–4.

46. 23 Weekly Comp. Pres. Doc. 715 (June 29, 1987).
47. 133 Cong. Rec. S. 8438 (June 23, 1987).
48. *Syracuse Peace Council* v. *WTVH (TV),* 809 F.2d 863 (1987).
49. *Meredith Corp.* v. *FCC,* 809 F.2d 863 (1987).
50. *Syracuse Peace Council* v. *Television Station WTVH,* 99 FCC 2d 1389 (1984).
51. *Red Lion, supra,* 388.
52. Id., 389.
53. "TRAC," *supra,* 506–7.
54. *Branch* v. *FCC,* 824 F.2d 37, 49–50 (D.C. Cir. 1987); *cert den.,* 56 U.S.L.W. 5623 (1988).
55. S. Rept. No. 100-34 on S. 742, 100th Cong., 1st sess. (1987); H. Rept. No. 100-108, Fairness in Broadcasting Act of 1987, 100th Cong., 1st sess. (1987).
56. *Syracuse Peace Council* v. *FCC,* 867 F.2d 654 (D.C. Cir. 1989).

Chapter 5

══════

1. Shepherd.
2. Much of the material in this part of Chapter 5 is based on Carson's *The Roguish World of Doctor Brinkley.*
3. *KFKB Broadcasting Ass'n., Inc.* v. *FRC,* 47 F.2d, 670, 671 (1931).
4. *FRC Annual Report,* 1931, 67–68.
5. *Broadcasting,* Oct. 15, 1932, 6.
6. Carson, 197.
7. Carson, 249–50.
8. Hoffer, 568–78; see also, *Hygeia,* May 1930; May 1932.
9. Id., 577–78.

Chapter 6

══════

1. Barnouw, I, 180.
2. The facts about Shuler are based largely on the opinion of the U.S. Court of Appeals for the D.C. Circuit cited in Note 3; an article in the *American Mercury* of December 1930 by Duncan Aikman, titled "Sayonarola in Los

Angeles" and an article in the *New Republic* of December 9, 1931, by Edmund Wilson.

3. *Trinity Methodist Church South* v. *FRC,* 62 F.2d 850 (1932); *cert. den.*, 288 U.S. 599 (1933).

4. Id., 853.

5. Much of the material about Father Coughlin is based on *Father Coughlin* by Sheldon Marcus.

6. *Encyclopedia Americana,* Vol. 8, p. 84.

7. *Great Lakes, supra.*

8. United Television Co., Inc., 55 FCC 2d 416 (1975); *recon. den.*, 59 FCC 2d 663 (1976); *aff'd. sub nom. United Broadcasting Co., Inc.* v. *FCC,* 565 F.2d 699 (1977); *cert. den.*, 434 U.S. 1046 (1978).

9. Id., 441.

10. Id., 441–42.

11. Id., 423.

12. 44 RR 2d, 1363 (1981).

13. Id., 1375–6.

14. Section 1343 of the criminal code provides a prison term of up to five years and/or a fine of up to one thousand dollars for obtaining money under false pretenses "by means of wire, radio or television communication."

15. Faith Center, Inc., 69 FCC 2d 1123 (1978); 82 FCC 2d 1 (1980); 83 FCC 2d 401 (1980); 84 FCC 2d 542 (1981); 86 FCC 2d 891 (1981); 88 FCC 2d 788 (1981); 90 FCC 2d 519 (1982); 92 FCC 2d 1255 (1983); 94 FCC 2d 756 (1983).

16. FCC Press Release, Dec. 8, 1982, Report No. 18597.

17. Joint dissent attached to Press Release, *supra.*

18. Id., p. 8.

19. *Time,* Aug. 3, 1987, 48–55.

20. 24 FCC 2d 18, 34–35 (1970); *recon. den.*, 27 FCC 2d 565 (1971).

21. 473 F.2d 16 (1972).

Chapter 7

1. Broadcasting Publications, Inc., *supra,* 61.

2. Id., 55. See also, Barnouw, II, 173–78.

3. 23 FCC 2d 880 (1970).

4. *NAB* v. *FCC,* 554 F.2d 1118 (1976).

5. Broadcasting Publications, Inc., *supra,* 196.

6. 22 FCC 2d 424 (1970).

7. *Citizen's Communications Center* v. *FCC,* 447 F.2d 1202 (1971).

8. Schwartz, 91–95.

9. Id., 179.
10. Id., 81.
11. Told to the author by Joseph Baudino, for many years vice-president of Westinghouse in Washington.
12. Dawson Nail, executive editor of *Television Digest,* says it was he, a reporter for *Broadcasting* magazine at the time, who unearthed and first published the story of Harris's interest in KRBB-TV.
13. Schwartz, 111.
14. Id., 103.
15. Id., 104–6.
16. Id., 106–9.
17. 47 U.S.C. 508; 74 Stat. 889 (1960).
18. 47 U.S.C. 509; 74 Stat. 889 (1960).

Chapter 8

▬▬▬▬

1. Sections 308(b) and 310(b), Title 47 U.S.C.
2. *American College Dictionary.*
3. Report, Order and Statement in the Matter of Policy Regarding Character Qualifications in Broadcast Licensing, 102 FCC 2d 1179, 1183 (1985); *recon. den.,* 62 RR 2d 619.
4. 32 FCC 689 (1962).
5. Transfer of Broadcast Facilities, Report and Order in BC Docket No. 81-897, FCC 82-519, 52 RR 2d 1081 (1982); *aff'd.,* Memorandum Opinion and Order, 99 FCC 2d 971 (1984).
6. *Anti-Trafficking in Broadcast Licenses.* Hearing before the Subcommittee on Telecommunications and Finance of the Committee on Energy and Commerce, H. of Rep., 100th Cong. 1st sess. on H.R. 1187, June 17, 1987.
7. Committee for Full Value of Storer Communications, Inc., 101 FCC 2d 434 (1985); *aff'd. sub nom. Storer Communications, Inc.* v. *FCC,* 762 F.2d 436 (D.C. Cir. 1985).
8. *Policy Statement on Tender Offers and Proxy Contests,* 59 RR 2d 1536 (1986).
9. *Office of Communication of the United Church of Christ, et al.* v. *FCC,* 826 F.2d 101 (D.C. Cir. 1987).
10. In re Metromedia, Inc., 98 FCC 2d 300; *recon. den.* 56 RR 2d 1198; *aff'd. sub nom. California Association of the Physically Handicapped* v. *FCC,* 778 F.2d 823 (D.C. Cir. 1985).
11. Letter to William S. Paley, 1 FCC Rcd. 1025 (1986); *recon. den.,* 2 FCC Rcd. 2274 (1987).
12. Boyer, 313, 322, 326.

13. *Anti-Trafficking in Broadcast Licenses, supra,* 146.
14. *Broadcasting,* June 30, 1986, 27–30.
15. Notice of Inquiry and Proposed Rule-Making, 28 FCC 2d 368, 369–70 (1971).
16. Children's Television Report and Policy Statement, 50 FCC 2d 1, 11 (1974).
17. TV Programming for Children, Report and Order, 96 FCC 2d 634 (1984); *aff'd. sub nom. Action for Children's Television* v. *FCC,* 756 F.2d 899 (D.C. Cir. 1985); Television Deregulation, Memorandum Opinion and Order, 104 FCC 2d 358 (1986).
18. *Action for Children's Television* v. *FCC,* 821 F.2d 741 (D.C. Cir. 1987).
19. *Washington Post,* June 9, Nov. 6, 1988.
20. Elimination of Unnecessary Broadcast Regulation, 94 FCC 2d 619 (1983); Report and Order in the Matter of Elimination of Unnecessary Broadcast Regulation, adopted Aug. 8, 1984, FCC 84-388, 49 Fed. Reg. 33264, 8-22-84; Policy Statement and Order in the Matter of Elimination of Unnecessary Broadcast Regulation, MM Docket 83-842, FCC 85-25, 34599, adopted Jan. 18, 1985.
21. Report of Congressional Research Service, Library of Congress, to House Committee on Energy and Commerce, Subcommittee on Telecommunications and Finance, Feb. 1, 1988.
22. News release, May 10, 1988, Telecommunications Subcommittee, *supra.*

Bibliography

Much of the material in this book is based on the author's personal experiences while associated with the National Broadcasting Company and the Federal Communications Commission and on information furnished by fellow and former staff members and acquaintances in the communications field. The remainder is derived from the official records of the FCC, Congress and the courts, the published works of individual authors, and trade publications such as *Broadcasting, Television/Radio Age,* and *TV Digest.*

The most frequently cited sources are the *Communications Act of 1934* (47 U.S.C.); the *Federal Communications Commission Reports* and, since Oct. 1, 1986, its successor, *The FCC Record;* the *United States Reports,* which contains the decisions of the U.S. Supreme Court; the *Federal Reporter,* in which the decisions of the U.S. circuit courts of appeal are published; the *United States Code;* the *Federal Register;* and the *Congressional Record.* Some of the legal citations are to a privately published compendium of FCC decisions, Pike & Fischer *Radio Regulation.*

Aikman, Duncan. "Sayonarola in Los Angeles." *American Mercury,* December 1930.

Americana Corporation. *Encyclopedia Americana.* New York: Americana Corporation, 1975.

American College Dictionary. New York: Random House, 1955.

Anderson, Kent. *Television Fraud.* Westport, Conn.: Greenwood Press, 1978.

Barnouw, Erik. *A History of Broadcasting in the United States,* 3 vols. New York: Oxford University Press, 1966–70.

Barrett, Marvin, and Zachary Sklar. *The Eye of the Storm (7th Alfred I. duPont-Columbia University Survey of Broadcast Journalism).* New York: Lippincott & Crowell, 1980.

Boyer, Peter J. *Who Killed CBS?* New York: Random House, 1988.

Broadcasting Publications, Inc. *The First Fifty Years of Broadcasting.* Washington, D.C.: Broadcasting Publications, Inc., 1982.

Broadcasting-Telecasting Yearbook. Washington, D.C.: Broadcasting Publications, Inc. (annual)

Broadcasting Yearbook. Washington, D.C.: Broadcasting Publications, Inc. (annual)

Brown, Les. *Les Brown's Encyclopedia of Television.* New York: Zoetrope, 1982.

Campbell, Robert. *The Golden Years of Broadcasting.* New York: Scribner's, 1976.

Carson, Gerald. *The Roguish World of Doctor Brinkley.* New York: Rinehart & Co., 1960.

Chase, Francis. *The Sound and the Fury: An Informal History of Broadcasting.* New York: Harper & Bros., 1942.

Cole, Barry, and Mal Ottinger. *The Reluctant Regulators.* Reading, Mass.: Addison-Wesley, 1978.

Crowell-Collier Publishing Co. *Collier's Magazine.* New York: Crowell-Collier Publishing Co. (weekly)

Dugger, Ronnie. *The Politician.* New York: W. W. Norton, 1982.

Efron, Edith. *The News Twisters.* Los Angeles: Nash, 1971.

_____. *How CBS Tried to Kill a Book.* Los Angeles: Nash, 1972.

Epstein, Edward Jay. *Between Fact and Fiction—The Problem of Journalism.* New York: Vintage Books, 1975.

Federal Radio Commission. *Annual Report to Congress.* Washington, D.C.: U.S. Government Printing Office, 1928–34.

Friendly, Fred W. *Due to Circumstances Beyond Our Control.* New York: Random House, 1967.

_____. *The Good Guys, The Bad Guys and the First Amendment.* New York: Random House, 1976.

Geller, Henry. *The Fairness Doctrine in Broadcasting.* Los Angeles: Rand, 1973.

Haddon, Jeffrey K., and Charles E. Schwann. *Prime-Time Preachers.* Reading, Mass.: Addison-Wesley, 1981.

Head, Sydney W., and Christopher H. Sterling. *Broadcasting in America.* Boston: Houghton Mifflin, 1987.

Hofstetter, C. Richard. *Bias in the News.* Columbus, Ohio: Ohio State Univ. Press, 1976.

Hygeia, May 1930 and May 1932.

Kahn, Frank J. *Documents of American Broadcasting.* 3rd ed. Englewood Cliffs, N.J.: Prentice-Hall, Inc., 1978.

Keeley, Joseph. *The Left-Leaning Antenna.* New Rochelle, N.Y.: Arlington House, 1971.

Krasnow, Erwin G., and Lawrence D. Longley. *The Politics of Broadcast Regulation.* New York: St. Martin's Press, 1973.

Lashner, Marilyn A. *The Chilling Effect in TV News.* New York: Praeger, 1984.

Lichty, Lawrence, and Malachi C. Topping. *American Broadcasting.* New York: Hastings House, 1975.

Marcus, Sheldon. *Father Coughlin.* Boston: Little Brown & Co., 1973.

Mayer, Martin. *About Television.* New York: Harper & Row, 1972.

Minow, Newton N. *Equal Time.* New York: Athaeneum, 1964.

Pusateri, C. Joseph. *Enterprise in Radio: WWL and the Business of Broadcasting in America.* Washington, D.C.: University Press of America, 1980.

Quinlan, Sterling. *The Hundred-Million Dollar Lunch.* Chicago: J. Phillip O'Hara, Inc., 1974.

RTNDA Communicator, October 1983, p. 28.

Schmeckebier, Lawrence R. *The Federal Radio Commission: Its History, Activities and Organization.* Washington, D.C.: Brookings Institution, 1932.

Schwartz, Bernard. *The Professor and the Commissions.* New York: Alfred A. Knopf, 1959.

Shayon, Robert Lewis. *The Crowd-Catchers.* New York: Saturday Review Press, 1973.

Simmons, Steven J. *The Fairness Doctrine and the Media.* Berkeley: University of California Press.

Skornia, Henry J., and Jack William Kitson. *Problems and Controversies in Television and Radio.* Palo Alto, Calif.: Pacific Books, 1968.

Small, William J. *To Kill a Messenger.* New York: Hastings House, 1970.

Sobol, Robert. *The Manipulators.* Garden City, N.Y.: Anchor Press/ Doubleday, 1976.

Sterling, Christopher H., and John M. Kittross. *Stay Tuned: A Concise History of American Broadcasting.* Belmont, Calif.: Wadsworth, 1978.

Time Magazine, Aug. 3, 1977, pp. 48–55.

U.S. Department of Commerce. *Radio Service Bulletins.* Washington, D.C.: U.S. Government Printing Office, 1912–27.

Washington Post, June 9, November 6, 1988.

Wilson, Edmund. *New Republic,* December 9, 1931.

Index